REPETITION

The Simple Truth for Old Souls in New Times

Doyle Moore

Copyright © 2024 Doyle Moore

All rights reserved

The characters and events portrayed in this book are fictitious. Any
similarity to real persons, living or dead, is coincidental and not intended
by the author.

No part of this book may be reproduced, or stored in a retrieval system,
or transmitted in any form or by any means, electronic, mechanical,
photocopying, recording, or otherwise, without express written
permission of the publisher.

ISBN-13: 9798335920766

Cover design by: Doyle, Will and Jessica
Library of Congress Control Number: 2018675309
Printed in the United States of America

for Juliet

CONTENTS

Title Page

Copyright

Dedication

Preface and Introduction 1

One -- Brainwashing 9

Two -- Pseudo-Reality 22

Three -- Beliefs 41

Four -- New Creation Myth 49

Five -- Reincarnation and Predetermination 62

Six -- Self-Brainwashing Rituals 73

Seven -- Creative Communication 90

Eight -- Consciousness 100

Nine -- Relearning How to Communicate 104

Ten -- Distractions 119

Eleven -- Primary Belief Systems 126

Twelve -- Secondary Belief Systems 143

Thirteen -- Creating a Future Vision 180

Fourteen -- Creating New Belief Systems 194

Author's Afterword 208

PREFACE AND INTRODUCTION

Preface

After recovering from three decades of religionism, the first half of which included weekly indoctrination, the second half was trying to make sense of their human owner's manual, and then a friend led me to a few books that allowed me to become what we called spiritually enlightened. The truths I took away from that part of my life include reincarnation, a single consciousness, and the concept that we are influencing our reality (or lack thereof) with our three creative tools: thought, word, and action.

After a few years and a handful of books about spirituality I realized I was not learning what I wanted to know. How can I make sense of everything and create happiness and bliss on a constant basis? I eventually realized that each time I eliminated what I now see as distractions, my life improved. If I stop watching television shows and commercials my life gets better. If I stop listening to talking heads, even those I generally agree with, my life gets better. Avoid the news, if at all possible, my life gets better. I essentially became an electronic hermit for about two decades while the final pieces to the puzzle came to me.

My youngest son had a daughter, and I started writing my ideas for her. And then, the only good thing that I know of from covid happened. They closed down daycare centers, but didn't close down my son's work, which caused my being blessed with a 40-month gig watching my granddaughter full time every other week. Best job of my life so far. Our goal every day was to always have fun and lots of eye contact. We enjoyed near daily walks, helping with meal preparation and chores, plus daily rituals including gratitude, affirmations, intentions, and meditation where we lit a candle that she eventually became in charge of; oh, we also enjoyed the playground monkey bars and the coffeehouse hot cocoa where they loved the neighborhood flowers she brought regularly.

In the last five years before starting this book I experienced a three-year period of less than perfect health. Even though the illness was the worst of my life, I was quite okay with it while staying in my happiness and bliss throughout. Quite a while before the illness I had come to fervently know that I am an eternal being and death is simply a shedding of my current meatsuit and is a process of going home or returning to my natural habitat. During my illness, while in the least pleasant condition, I sought out positive distractions on the common internet sources and discovered the last piece of the puzzle to the formula for this pseudo reality which was what specifically beliefs are and how we get them and what they do.

It was about this time, I was ready to shed this meatsuit and go home, when I felt like I was given a choice to make, and a question came to me: do I have anything else I want to do before leaving this meatsuit and going home? And it came to me that I should finish the book I started over 25 years ago. That is why I am here now. Please enjoy what I hope for some of you, will positively change your life.

Introduction

"Repetition: The Simple Truth for Old Souls in New Times" provides the reader with a process to improve their life progressively each year, and some new ideas about how exactly this reality works including why and how everything is the way it is, including a plan to transform the world into the abundant, loving and peaceful reality it has always meant to be; and, inevitably will be. I provide my perspective on the concepts of the spirit world and reincarnation as they relate to the simple truths, herein. I also show how positivity works, dismantling many claims from existing belief systems in our current reality.

We each have the ability to be happy and in a state of bliss. As we learn how things currently work and start the process of focusing our personal creative energies and learn to avoid the overwhelming undesirable distractions that the general population of this planet endures constantly, we will experience the calm peace of mind leading to great improvements in our personal reality. As we gather with like-minded people, as we teach them what we like and they teach us what they like, in positive supportive collaboration we will build a powerful loving community together.

Using ancient wisdom and ideas from the greatest minds of our time I believe I have uncovered the missing link in the illusion of reality. That's right, the illusion of reality. We should believe science when it tells us that reality is 100% empty space, to over ten digits of accuracy, making what we believe to be reality nonexistent, or illusionary. It will become easy to imagine the process of how things got into this game and how the creation process has ignorantly been misused throughout history which has led to what I call parasitic beliefs, or aspects of reality that exist simply to support other aspects of reality because of our lack of understanding of how nothingness turns into something.

DOYLEMOORE

I've been told that every major religion throughout time includes the concept of a single consciousness, and I believe this is key to comprehending why this illusion of life exists. If it weren't for consciousness, we would have no experience of what we call reality, so consciousness must play a significant role in reality, since it would appear to be the only thing that is "real" in the misnomer we call "reality", for which I provide the simple formula for how this pseudo-reality works.

I have only had two visions in my life, so far. Both visions were of the same thing. The first was last century and the second was a couple years ago. These visions were about a meeting we all had prior to this lifetime that we are currently experiencing. The visions detailed what I believe is the real "second coming", where many old souls are born to help transform the game into the abundant, loving and peaceful pseudo-reality it has always meant to be and inevitably will be. There would be no reason for you to be reading this if you were not at this meeting, prior to your birth; so, you were at the meeting too, believe it or not.

I believe it is important to get this message out as soon as possible so this book has neither been professionally edited, nor censored by any external sources. It is time for humans to grow out of our cocoon and transform into the butterflies that we are – it is natural and ultimately inevitable. Get the fuck over it and please read this book.

Repetition is all you need to create whatever you can imagine.

After I wrote the above pitch, a wise friend provided me with this:

Hey Doyle! I'm guessing this pitch is for a potential publisher? I drafted up a new version that's geared towards a publisher. I tried to make it super concise. Hope this helps!

Book Title: "Repetition: The Simple Truth for Old Souls in New Times"

In a world saturated with spiritual platitudes and self-help gurus, "Repetition" emerges as a stark, unflinching examination of reality itself. This isn't just another book promising personal transformation—it's a radical deconstruction of existence that challenges readers to question everything they think they know about life, consciousness, and the nature of reality.

The author presents a captivating blend of ancient wisdom and cutting-edge thought, proposing a revolutionary formula for how our pseudo-reality functions. Drawing on quantum physics, which tells us that reality is 99.9999999999% empty space, the book explores how our misunderstanding of this fundamental emptiness has led to what the author terms "parasitic beliefs"—ideas that exist solely to perpetuate themselves and our collective illusions.

Key features of "Repetition" include:

1. A no-nonsense approach to personal growth that promises real, measurable improvement year after year.
2. A fresh perspective on spirituality that dismantles common beliefs while offering a more grounded alternative.
3. An exploration of the "single consciousness" concept found in major religions, reframed through a lens of modern understanding.
4. A unique take on reincarnation and the idea of "old souls," including the author's personal visions of a pre-birth gathering of many old souls.
5. Practical techniques for focusing creative energies and avoiding societal distractions, leading to greater peace of mind and personal fulfillment.

Doyle Moore's voice is unapologetically direct at times provocative, but always in service of uncovering deeper truths. This raw, unfiltered approach to profound philosophical

DOYLEMOORE

concepts will resonate with readers tired of sugar-coated spirituality and hungry for authentic insights.

"Repetition" is poised to spark controversy and conversation in equal measure. It's a book for the seekers, the skeptics, and anyone brave enough to question the nature of their own existence. In a market flooded with rehashed ideas, this book stands out for its original thought, challenging readers to wake up to the reality behind the illusion.

This is more than a book—it's a call to action for those ready to transcend the limitations of conventional thinking and step into a new paradigm of understanding. "Repetition" promises to be the philosophical equivalent of a cold shower: shocking, invigorating, and ultimately cleansing.

End of a lovely, well-written pitch by my good friend Will Zesiger.

This is a good place to point out that I am a shitty writer. I just say whatever comes to mind usually and hope I can make sense of it later, and sometimes it doesn't make sense later and I'll have to toss it out but only a few times, so I keep throwing words at the keyboard and hope something sticks. Hope you can endure 60,000+ words of this shit; thank you very much for reading it.

There are no facts in this book, everything herein is the imagination of the author. It should be believed, if, and only if the reader finds that it feels good or right to consider believing in and only believe the stuff you like. Just don't blame me if you aren't getting desired results if you choose to disbelieve some of the good stuff, but anything in here that you believe can still help — whatever catches your interests. As for there being no facts in this book, facts aren't really facts – they don't empirically exist. Since time is an illusion and the only ultimate truth is change, nothing is necessarily going to stay a fact. Facts are only facts if you personally believe in them. We each have our own personal truth, and with it an individual set of facts unique to each person. To impose new facts on others doesn't seem to be the thing to do because facts are subject to change with new information and the personal information that one has is a brainwashed result. I'm saying this because it's easy to make up evidence of any type that someone wants – it only needs to be believed in to become real. (If I'm lucky others will create evidence that what I say in the book is completely wrong. This will add to the argument that what I'm talking about has merit, or you wouldn't hear anything about it.) I shall describe the process in detail—it happens all the time, whatever a few people believe is real starts to become real, and the more people that believe it makes it more real, whatever it is it starts showing up in reality, every fucking time.

Allow me to say that everything in this book was at the time I wrote it, my truth. There is no guarantee that I won't change my mind, after all, the only ultimate truth is change. Do not blindly believe anything in this book that doesn't resonate as something for you. I also wouldn't blindly believe anything – even things you already believe in, believe what feels best to you, and be willing to change your beliefs as new information warrants change.

I do not expect anyone to agree with everything in this book, but I ask that you consider all the different things I'm saying to see what works for you.

Post-Introduction Advertisement

September 2024.

I'm just adding the final touches to this book, but I need to include this part, just in case this thing isn't to the quality of what you hoped it would be. Sorry about all the rambling but I am going to ramble some more now.

In this book that you are about to read, I have simplified (or redefined) Shadow Work, Beliefs, Brainwashing, Reality (or the lack thereof), Consciousness, Reincarnation, Process Engineering (or at least, "the big red X" for which I share the two most critical things to focus collective creation efforts on), the Second Coming, a number of other things, how to make your life better each year, and how and why we are all here. (Yeah, I know, "one crazy mo-fo", that's what you might be thinking.) (Imagine what I'm thinking. What the hell am I doing? If I thought this incessant need to write this shit would go away, I don't know if I would risk losing friends and alienating those, I love dearly by writing this message; if only I had any other choice.) (This inevitable world transformation into a peaceful loving abundant reality, is underway. Many people are called to participate but some of us haven't been shown how reality works yet. Hopefully the ideas I'm sharing will help us move past the barrage of distractions caused by repetitive message brainwashing.)

Again, I would like to apologize for the lack of professionalism I assume will be present in this book. Even though I have had much help from friends with this work, I had hoped to find someone to magically help finish this thing, but the universe has seen fit to instill an urgency of completion and dissemination of this message. And, the way I write, albeit potentially driving would be editors insane with my natural writing/talking style, there may well be purpose behind my style that isn't apparent. Perhaps there are subtle brainwashing effects from the extra words that I include that an editor is ripping his hair out saying, "extra unnecessary words" and I'm thinking potential brainwashing improvement, for the right people. Idk, but you're all stuck for the ride now, hope you have some fun reading this. If anything doesn't make sense please read it over carefully, every word, again, until it does. It's okay if you spend more time having to figure out what the hell I'm saying, because I'm saying some new stuff that you may need a minute to digest – after all my mission is to brainwash you into believing something likely completely different than ever before. Thank you.

ONE -- BRAINWASHING

Pre-E1 Brainwashing Commercial

Repetition

WE REPEAT OURSELVES
by 3 Hand Stephen

this is a mission of repetition
this is a mission of repetition
this is a mission of repetition

we repeat ourselves; we repeat ourselves

questa è una missione di ripetizione
questa è una missione di ripetizione
questa è una missione di ripetizione

we repeat ourselves; we repeat ourselves

c'est une mission de répétition
c'est une mission de répétition
c'est une mission de répétition

we repeat ourselves; we repeat ourselves

WE REPEAT OURSELVES

Episode 1 Brainwashing You

Repetition is what controls reality. The more times something enters our consciousness the bigger portion of our lives it has. This is both on a population and at a personal level. You control a population by repeating the same thing over and over, and too really sink your teeth in, repeat the same thing from different places so it isn't associated with you. We call this good marketing. I call this brainwashing. We need help to change the world, but we don't need help to change ourselves.

Repetition works on a personal level, also. We will learn here how to gain influence over our personal reality and be able to experience happiness and bliss as we learn to avoid repetition of things that we do not want more of in our reality. We may hopefully learn how to experience the difference between knowing something and constantly thinking about it. I believe it is important to learn to focus on things we want more of rather than the things we do not want. Focusing on the solution, not the problem, is the goal to start any lasting change. You will never get something to go away if you keep talking or thinking about it.

I use the process of repetitive messaging, aka brainwashing, in some new ways for nonfiction books. It is common to repeat things in slightly different ways to get a point across, but for some reason, unlike lyrics, poetry and advertising, to say the same exact thing over and over is frowned upon. I apologize if this is bothersome to you, but please, if possible, please read it anyway even though you just did – it's the brainwashing effect that I'm after.

Both "beliefs" and "brainwashing", for many people, have very squishy definitions, but for the purpose of this book (and until you find a better more useful definition), please re-define them this way:

Beliefs are repetitive thoughts and repetitive words.

Brainwashing is repetitive thoughts and repetitive words.

That was easy. But likely not enough. The definitions above are the most accurate but people tend to want to complicate things, which is a huge distraction and waste of time and creative energy.

More specifically, your personal beliefs are nothing more or less than your repetitive thoughts and your repetitive words.

More specifically, brainwashing is any messaging received into the mind, consciously and subconsciously, and becomes a thought. External messages are imposed thoughts which upon repetition, become beliefs, given the new definition of beliefs above. Internal, self-brainwashing are chosen messages that we choose to brainwash ourselves with to direct and produce a chosen reality, like intentions and affirmations. On the other hand, anything we spend our time thinking or saying repetitively is also brainwashing and will become beliefs – both thinking and saying are our personal responsibility and critical to improve your reality and to understand what's going on here.

We seem to complicate things by trying to explain something that doesn't need to be explained or even considered as useful, once we understand how everything becomes a part of our personal and collective realities. The simplest answer is the solution. All the why's and how's are unnecessary and likely exist to appease the lack of understanding of how things get here in the first place.

Welcome to what could be the simplest explanation for everything in the universe that you will ever hear. It's so simple that I could tell you what it is in a page or two, but I won't make any money on a two page long book, so I'm also going to attempt to brainwash you into believing what I'm saying by using the very techniques used by most, if not all, of the different sources of brainwashing that we regularly experience. You may be under the misconception that we are not constantly being brainwashed by everything that we repeatedly hear, see, say, sense or experience. I am using a new twist on the concept of brainwashing, which by the name would imply either the cleaning off of something in the brain, or possibly by using a secondary definition of "wash" as in "white washing" which is what they used to call the process of painting a surface "white", covering up the natural color of something, like a fence, or in the case of brainwashing, covering up what something would naturally look like without the brainwashing.

A late friend of mine used to teach sales training and before he finally gave up trying to teach me how to sell something, he discovered that I have a horrible memory for almost everything that doesn't pertain to my personal truths, which can be a problem when others have expectations of how another human should act or be. He taught me that we can often remember things by a process he called spaced repetition. If we are exposed to something repeatedly, over time, we can usually remember it, with enough spaced repetition. This process is very effective to get humans to buy things. My friend used to say that the first time someone hears something, they usually reject the idea because they have never heard it before. The second time they hear it, they think, "I've heard that before"; and, after they have heard it three or more times, their likelihood of investing in the idea goes up considerably. The process of spaced repetition is a subtle yet very effective, and profitable, means of brainwashing. Yeah, yeah, all you salespeople should not get your panties in a bunch – this is just an emotional response that indicates that this is actually something you can learn something useful from, which is a great lead-in for an introduction to the process of Shadow Work.

Shadow work explains why humans get upset after hearing, seeing or experiencing something specific. Unless your life mission is involved, if something that you see, hear or read strikes an emotional chord, be it positive or negative, this is consciousness or your Higher Self trying to show you something about yourself that you currently do not realize. There are like a gazillion things out there that can piss people off, but only a relatively small amount of these things strikes an emotional chord in any one person – these things are about the person who gets pissed off. If I am upset about something, it is all about me – no one else, nothing to blame but my misconception about myself.

I tend to digress to clarify or explain something and when I get done with the explanation, I have to go back to the topic that led to the digression in the first place. I'm afraid you may have to endure my digressions, and I will try not to leave you hanging when I'm done with them – it is often like climbing out of a proverbial rabbit hole. So, anyway, I was trying to tell you what I'm up to in this book. First, I would like to explain how reality works and what is really going on here in this game of make believe, this life you are living now in the Earth Space Time Continuum, which I will also refer to as the ESTC. And, secondly, to do this, I am planning to use the same type of repetitive messaging that most of us experience all the time, and I call this brainwashing. So, technically, I'm going to brainwash you the best I can, and I mean "the best" in two ways. First, I'm going to brainwash you with a revolutionary idea that is so simple that many may not believe it is true until I brainwash you with the new simple idea for a few thousand words of repetitive messaging, also known as brainwashing; and, secondly, but at the same time, demonstrate how exactly we are being brainwashed and how to recognize and avoid undesired brainwashing in the future. Unlike most brainwashing, or repetitive messaging, that we experience, the purpose of my efforts is not to get anything out of you or control you but to show you how and why we believe all the undesirable stuff that we currently believe, while sharing the secrets to being happy and transforming both your personal and collective realities into a better reality that you choose to experience, the way you choose to experience it, at least your personal reality (we have no control over others, only intentions).

Throughout this book I use repetitive messaging as brainwashing to help you, the reader, remember the main points of the message along with examples from common belief systems, as well as exercises or repetitive processes to help you incorporate these new ideas into your everyday life, into your reality. Yes, I intend to brainwash you to think a new thought about reality but unlike the constant brainwashing that we allow into our mind in current modern society, I have no ulterior motivation other than to show you that we are constantly brainwashed by every repetitive message that we allow to continue into our mind, particularly those that have us repetitively speaking their message. I don't need you to do anything for my survival – unlike every commercial enterprise, most educational or entertainment sources and everything from both primary and secondary belief systems that currently provide messaging to exist in our reality – they need us, but we do not need them; if we don't sense (hear, see, etcetera) their message than it does not impact us, and eventually may not even exist to us.

Besides repetitive messaging I'm going to brainwash you with advertising methods also. The most effective way to sell something is repetitively forcing a message into a population's awareness by way of advertisement like was originally started with newspaper, magazine, radio and television commercials or advertisements, and has been propagated into online portals, email, and most any way unrequested, or ignorantly requested, messaging can be imposed on the target population, be it for sales or simply to change or enhance beliefs.

And now, for a short message from our sponsors:

Just a quick warning about the advertisements or commercials in between chapters in this book. There may be some foul language in these "AD's" because they are from presentations I made while outlining the book, but if foul language offends you more than what the book is saying, perhaps "fuck" is your first shadow to work on.

Post-E1.1 Brainwashing Commercial Saint Albert

St Albert/Reality Rev3.1 (GD=granddaughter; Me=me)

This talk is part of something that I titled "Saint Albert and reality, or lack thereof "

Albert Einstein says, and I quote...

GD: Grandpa, my daddy said that Frankenstein is a made-up monster for scary movies and that you are nuts and to not believe the crazy shit you say.

Me: That sounds like your daddy – both my kids think I'm

DOYLEMOORE

nuts, but you can lead a horse to water but you…

GD: Grandpa, we're not talking about horses. You're avoiding the question. Who cares what a movie monster says, in the first place? Why are you quoting it?

Me: I'm not sure where you got Frankenstein from, but I was talking about Albert Einstein not Frankenstein. Einstein is arguably one of the smartest scientific minds ever. Can I go on?

GD: I guess. I just thought I should warn everyone that you may be nuts. It's nothing personal, grandpa.

Me: Thank you, my dear. It's probably a valid warning.

anyway,

Albert Einstein says, and I quote: "Concerning matter, we have been all wrong. What we have called matter is energy, whose vibration has been so lowered as to be perceptible to the senses. Matter is spirit reduced to (the) point of visibility. There is no matter." End quote.

Another Einstein quote: "Time and space are not conditions in which we live, but modes by which we think. Physical concepts are free creations of the human mind, and are not, however it may seem, determined by the external world."

Here is one last Einstein quote: "Reality is merely an illusion, albeit a very persistent one."

GD: Grandpa, this Frankenstein guy sounds nuttier than you do.

Me: Thank you, dear. That puts me in good company.

Science tells us that everything is made of atoms and atoms are 100% empty space, mathematically, to more than ten digits of accuracy.

That means that our perception of reality is completely fucked up—reality is more like a pseudo reality or an illusion. There is nothing real in what we call reality, even us.

First and foremost, there is nothing real in what we perceive as reality— there is nothing here. Quantum mathematicians have concluded some time ago that when they add everything up in reality that the sum total of everything equals zero.

What can possibly make all this nothingness appear and function like somethingness? What makes nothing into something? This question has not been answered within science, or any other belief system, since it all began. Nor do we seem any closer to finding out as long as we keep ignoring that it is all an illusion, and nothing is here. This is not a process that humans currently appear to understand, AT ALL!

Until we understand the process of turning nothingness into somethingness, we really don't know what the fuck is going on here. And until we understand how to make the somethingness into something that we desire to experience, we have no control over what we experience,

Again, our conscious mind asks, what is going on here, and why?

This meatsuit that you find yourself in, doesn't exist which means you are not your body; but you are conscious and consciousness. As you go through your day, try to remember that there is nothing, NOTHING, here?

GD: Grandpa, why do you waste everyone's time when you could literally have been done after four words, "there is nothing here". Be done already
Me: Sorry, I'll be done in a few more words.

Consciousness is common to all experience.

I believe that our Beliefs are involved in all this. I have developed a theory of reality that explains everything that I plan to share with you, but I don't have time today...

In higher mathematics the solution is rarely a number. When there are variables at play the solution is to simplify the formula. We eliminate variables that don't really affect the end result until the formula or equation is as easy to understand, with as few variables as possible. That is what I have done with

DOYLEMOORE

my formula for reality...

> GD: *Grandpa, please just shut the fuck up.*
> Me: *Okay,*

Thank you.

Post-E1.2 Brainwashing Commercial
Nothing at all

The following is from other readings:

If nothing is here at all, how come there are so many things that we think are here?

Yes, that's right: there are so many things that we think are here. Or, maybe to put it more clearly, many things are here because we think them here; or we think them and the illusion of them appears within this ESTC to the level that we know they exist.

Until we understand the process of turning nothingness into somethingness, we really don't know what the fuck is going on here. And until we understand how to make the somethingness into something that we desire to experience, we have no control over what we experience,

Consciousness is common to all experience. We cannot observe or experience anything without consciousness. We have no actual evidence that things unperceived or unobserved in some way, even exist. Maybe they don't. Maybe that's why atoms seem to bounce around the universe all the time. If an atom is not needed for the illusion that consciousness is creating, why would it be here — why would it exist, since nothing is here anyway.

Science tells us that nothing is here – atoms are 100% empty space to over ten digits of accuracy – but for some reason it slipped their mind to tell us this – that means there isn't a fucking thing here, GTFOI

So, nothing is here. It seems the question we should ask is, "how do we, or what is the process to, turn nothing into something?" How did this illusion of gazillions of somethings get here considering there isn't actually a damn thing here?

Hopefully, even if you're just humoring me, you will say, "that's a good question, Doyle?"

<pause and listen for responses, reply if needed>

Thank you, even if you are just humoring the old guy – that's very nice of you.

It's vital to understand that there has never been anything here to discover, there is nothing here. Not only when something is thought to have been discovered, but also when we later see evidence of where it came from or how it works, it came from nothingness and consciousness, and it works just the way we think it does; yes, you can prove it to me but how did your proof turn from nothing into something? There isn't anything here.

Since, by definition, if nothing is here than there is nothing here to discover, period! I like to refer to the expert, Albert Einstein, "Physical concepts are the free creations of the human mind, and are not, however it may seem, determined by the external world"

We have this whole reality thing completely backwards. We think something is here and has always been that way when we are actually thinking it into the illusion of both physicality and its cause – there is no physicality since there is nothing here and it is here just because. "Be-cause" is another way of saying it is caused by your being; and, this is similar to the word, "believe", which is us leaving things here that appear real with our being – "be-lieving" things into being.

In higher mathematics the solution is rarely a number.

When there are variables at play the solution is to simplify the formula. This process is often tedious when there's more than a few variables. One tries to eliminate variables that don't really affect the end result until the formula or equation is as easy to understand, with as few variables as possible. That is what I have done with my formula for reality.

Again, science tells us that everything is made of atoms and atoms are 100% empty space, mathematically, to over ten digits of accuracy. There is nothing real in what we call reality, even us; and again, quantum brainiacs have concluded that when they add everything up in reality the sum total of everything is nothing.

We will never see unexpected data. If we believe everything is the way it is and there is little or nothing, we can do to influence it, than we will not see anything outside of our beliefs, especially what I'm saying, that we are in fact manifesting everything, including the data that supports what we believe, as well as our personal and collective realities. This means if you believe something is impossible and fervently know it cannot exist, you will not see any evidence that it does exist. So please have an open mind and ponder the possibility, not a perceived impossibility.

My formula for reality, after removing all unnecessary variables, is a simple equation that, once it is believed, works every time and we will see it at work everywhere, all around us, constantly; and we will understand why many things happen to people and we can often predict what is likely to happen by what they say and do.

Your reality equals the product of your beliefs which are nothing more or less than all of your repetitive thoughts and repetitive words. Period.

So, everything turns from nothing into something each instant, both collectively and individually, based on the beliefs of the individual and all the people in the collective of individuals. And beliefs are nothing more or less than one's repetitive thoughts and repetitive words. This is the first explanation that I have found that explains everything without any organization telling me what is real or unreal. Yes, that means this whole game of life is much easier to figure out since nothing is real, which means nothing is necessarily the way we were told it is, nothing at all.

Thank you.

TWO -- PSEUDO-REALITY

Episode 2 Reality (or the lack thereof)

Would you like to know what's really going on here?

What if everything is much easier and simpler than you have ever imagined?

What if you have full control of your personal reality including your happiness and comfort, and all you have to do is change your mind about it, control your words and minimize or eliminate undesired brainwashing?

The first thing that needs to be resolved before many of us can know what's really going on here is our beliefs about what is possible. A very common belief in humanity on this planet at this time is that nobody really knows what's going on here. Until we can accept or believe that, not only do some people know what's really going on here but that we can learn how and why everything is the way it is and how to start to influence our own personal reality, we will neither see a new way as worthwhile, nor can we see that it is working at all.

How can we accept a new idea that we don't believe in? How can we possibly believe in something we consider impossible? We cannot. Herein may be your first challenge: expand your personal "realm of possibility".

We must first believe something is possible before we will see what we think is evidence of it in our reality. To see that this is true, all you need to do is observe people that believe differently than you do. For example, if you do not believe in religion, it becomes obvious, upon observation, that some of the things religionists believe in and because they do believe, their reality shows them evidence of it being real. Some things in a religionist's reality are not true for you, even if you resonate with some of their beliefs like the concept of the golden rule or the value of loving your neighbors, there are still many things completely unbelievable, obviously unproductive, and are not things you can condone as useful in any way, like rituals where they drink the blood and eat the body of a christ that died and after which he still walked the earth – it's hard to take seriously a group that condones vampires, cannibalism and zombie leaders, even if these things do make entertaining movies. But the point is that these people are obviously experiencing a completely different reality than you are – they actually believe the whole purpose of life is to live in fear and jump through a constantly moving hoop, over time, in order to deserve eternal life when they die, or more importantly to avoid an eternal damnation in hell; when, obviously, there is no hell unless you don't know that there is no hell. Again, the point being, our reality looks just as absurd to them as their reality looks to us; and, I'm kind of stuck in the middle here because I see all your current belief systems as completely unproductive and riddled with un-useful concepts given how your primary belief system has no explanation for how things become things when there is nothing here to begin with, as well as no logical reason for humanity to exist at all.

To believe that something is possible that we do not currently believe we must first open our mind to new ideas that we do not currently believe are possible. This is done by expanding what I call one's "realm of possibilities".

Everyone has a personal realm of possibilities which defines what you can and cannot observe in reality; and this means you will neither observe nor see any indication of things that you do not believe in. A great example of this is described in the book "Hawaii" by James Mitchener. In the book it details that the native Hawaiians' first encounter with large sailing vessels was when the first non-Hawaiians rowed their boats from the ship to the beach where natives were present. When asked how they had rowed so far across the seas the newcomers pointed to their ship in the bay and the natives could not see it. A ship that big was outside the natives' realm of possibility. They had never fathomed ships so large so they could not see what would later become obvious, once a few natives were taken back to the ship to experience it first-hand. Some fervent disbelievers would swim out and touch the ship to verify that it was in fact there.

The natives expanded their realm of possibility when presented with a creation that they could experience, firsthand.

If you have a hard time accepting new ideas, please say out loud at least once a day, "I am alert to the opportunity of improbable possibilities." This will help you be alert to things close to the edge of your current realm of possibilities. My plan, as I alluded to already, is to brainwash you into new ideas with repetitive messaging, so if you can, please allow the brainwashing to help expand your realm of possibilities,

Albert Einstein is arguably one of the greatest scientists ever. He was known for his intelligence and work in theoretical physics. Albert Einstein says, and I quote: "Concerning matter, we have been all wrong. What we have called matter is energy, whose vibration has been so lowered as to be perceptible to the senses. Matter is spirit reduced to (the) point of visibility. There is no matter." End quote.

Something I learned on my path from our most effective primary belief systems, science, was that atoms are virtually entirely empty space, from every personally verifiable perspective. Everything other than the general observation that nothing is here, is what I would label a myth, just as I would label it in any belief system.

By "primary belief system" I mean an organization whose only product or purpose is telling you what you should believe as truth – the three big primary belief systems are religion, science and spirituality. Education is the primary delivery system for subject-based brainwashing and is the most effective way to perpetuate specific historical creations to new humans – a dozen years of brainwashing for young meatsuits to see if you may be worth up to another dozen years of brainwashing, aka education, to make one worthy of higher social status and elevation, albeit minimal, in physical rewards, aka money.

I learned in prep school that everything in this reality is made of atoms. Although they told us at the time that atoms were 99.99999999999996% empty space, they never pointed

DOYLEMOORE

out the now obvious fact that this is 100.000000000000%, empty space which means there is nothing actually here. The 0.0000000000004% that's unaccounted for in the atom is information – the same thing as your thoughts, your consciousness; and is far too small of a fraction to physically verify with anything other than equipment and/or processes created with the intention of telling us what we think we need to know to verify the observation of our creation. I believe my breakfast cereal analogy applies here, which is quite hard to deny: if I have 0.0000000000004% of cereal left in the box, I don't have any cereal at all – plus I would wager there is far more cereal in the previously full, empty box than 0.0000000000004%.

(Anything that I cannot sense with my own meatsuit, doesn't impact my reality. Considering nothing is real, everything here is not really here; it's all an illusion. For example, I like electricity and the things it does for me, but I cannot sense it in any way unless I get too close and it can kill me, so I avoid it and other than that I don't need to think about it personally in any way that doesn't enhance my interaction with other people, unless there is something I would like more of in my reality, like clothes that would keep you at whatever temperature you like. But the point is, if it doesn't have something to do with me, that I can sense in some way, or something that I intend for my perfect reality, I don't believe that I am spending my creative energy in the wisest way that I can.)

Quantum mathematicians have added everything up in the universe, and the sum total of everything equals zero – another confirmation that there is nothing here. Since nothing is here, this raises the argument that this world, and everything here, is not real. There is nothing real in what we call reality. This, quite simply, means this world and everything in it, including you, is in fact, nothing more than illusion. This game we are playing here in the ESTC is more like a pseudo-reality than a reality since nothing is here.

Albert Einstein also told us, "Reality is merely an illusion, albeit a very persistent one."

One big unanswered question within our current belief systems, including science, is how exactly do we turn nothing into something? This is a process that is critical to understanding how this game works. We think all this stuff in the world, all the things we know about what's going on here, are real, but the conclusions of our wisest meatsuits, throughout time, firmly state that there isn't a damn thing here, so again, the formula for reality must include the process for turning nothing into something and making the something we turn it into something we consciously desire to experience.

Another Einstein quote: "Time and space are not conditions in which we live, but modes by which we think. Physical concepts are free creations of the human mind, and are not, however it may seem, determined by the external world."

In keeping with my general attempt to brainwash the reader, "Physical concepts are free creations of the human mind", "Physical concepts are free creations of the human mind", and "Physical concepts are free creations of the human mind". Repetition. Just a little more, "Physical concepts … are not, however it may seem, determined by the external world", "Physical concepts … are not, however it may seem, determined by the external world", and "Physical concepts … are not, however it may seem, determined by the external world". Thank you for reading this. To really maximize your brainwashing it is best to read it out loud.

The human mind, and not the external world, create physical concepts. From this, I have concluded that consciousness is not only the means by which we observe our creations, but consciousness is also the source of physicality because the only thing here is consciousness, since nothing is determined by the external world, aka nothing is here – at least nothing made of atoms, including us.

I asked some folks to read a rev0 and a dear friend, very versed in the ways of science and chemistry, responded to the idea that there is nothing here with a technical argument because there was mass so then there is actually something here. I should have just replied, we created a way to weigh, too, but I didn't think of that at the time and replied with this instead.

Start of reply to friend:

I am not making any claims to adhere to current organized sources of humans' truths or sources of facts, including religion, spiritual divinations, and science. I believe that they are all heavily laced with what I call parasitic beliefs that serve no constructive purpose and usually exist as "evidence" or "proof" of something that I believe is simply the result of humans' creation.

I believe everything in this illusion is the product of consciousness*, by definition.

The arguments made in the book are from things that have resonated with me as truths that consciousness has provided me with throughout my life's search for "what the fuck is really going on here, and why?" I have found these "truths" in many different places, many from the three primary sources of truths or facts. (Although these truths have been coming to me my whole life, they didn't all fit into a logical conclusion, until the last few years, providing me with the actual process by which humans have created, and continue to create their reality since before the concept of time.)

For example, the concept of a single consciousness, I've been told, is in all major religions throughout history, in one way or another. They call it different names and can give it very flawed characteristics associated with controlling populations often with fear-based propaganda. But the central theme is a single creative consciousness which resonates greatly with my understanding of why this illusion that we call life exists at all.

For another example, the concept that there is nothing here is from Albert Einstein quotes ("there is no matter", "this is all an illusion", (etc.)). Although it wasn't obvious to me when I was being educated (aka brainwashed) in the ways of science and mathematics, I now no longer see viability or personal usefulness to variables (or presumed constants) that dominate a formula, even for St Albert's contributions, like E=mc2**. Even though I no longer feel the need to personally think about and/or remember many things, I still highly value many of the scientific creations that can be useful within, what I am calling, an "imagineering" endeavor, freer from imposed limitations on possibilities than my twenty years in Engineering was.

*"everything ... is the product of consciousness" is asterisked because I am not limiting everything here to "human creation", and I don't know for sure about what I've heard called "higher evolved beings" (HEBs) and/or aliens from other planets and/or times, but I am not convinced they (HEBs+) are not also created by human consciousness (as well as the general conclusions we have regarding the universe, as we currently "know" it to be). I believe humans' creative energies (beliefs) would be more productively spent focusing our words and thoughts on things we desire more of in our reality – in the ESTC (earth space time continuum), as this is where consciousness is choosing to be while we are conscious (we can deal with other places/times when we are sleeping).

** too big or too small of a number, generally, is not useful or usable (without a created means of evaluation) from a human perspective in ESTC reality. For example, if I have 0.0000000004% of the cereal left in the box, I don't have any cereal at all.

End of reply to friend.

We are trained to mistakenly think that to know something requires experience-based evidence, but this is not the way it works. There is nothing here so what we are observing as evidence is actually the creation of our beliefs, which are nothing more or less than our repeated thoughts and words – we will get into this in detail shortly.

We must believe in something before we can see it. Belief

is the precursor to knowing. We cannot know anything before we believe in it.

Back to the issue at hand, what is the reason for this (earth space time continuum) ESTC illusion, what is the purpose of this illusion, and how does it work – what makes things the way they are? The reason for the illusion of physicality is directly tied to the concept of a single consciousness. The purpose of this illusion is companionship. How things become what they are, is defined in my formula for reality.

First, I would like you to expand your personal realm of possibility as far as you possibly can. You have a lot more influence over this pseudo reality than you likely have ever imagined. You control your personal reality and influence all of your collective realities up to and including the planetary collective of all the people on the planet. I should probably repeat the previous sentence a few dozen times to help brainwash you into believing it might be worth considering, in an attempt to enlarge your realm of possibility to include a new idea.

In higher mathematics the solution is rarely a number. When there are variables at play the solution is to simplify the formula. This process is often tedious when there's more than a few variables. One tries to eliminate variables that don't really affect the end result until the formula or equation is as easy to understand, with as few variables as possible. That is what I have done with my formula for reality.

Again, science tells us that everything is made of atoms and atoms are 100% empty space, mathematically, to over ten digits of accuracy. There is nothing real in what we call reality, even us; and again, quantum brainiacs have concluded that when they add everything up in reality the sum total of everything is nothing.

We will never see unexpected data. If we believe everything is the way it is and there is little or nothing, we can do to influence it, than we will not see anything outside of our beliefs, especially what I'm saying, that we are in fact manifesting everything, including the data that supports what we believe, as well as our personal and collective realities. This means you – if you believe something is impossible and fervently know it cannot exist, you will not see any evidence that it does exist – even a huge sailing vessel in the harbor. However, if you hear it repeatedly, after enough repetition your realm of possibility expands, often without being aware of it, at which time you may start to experience or sense evidence of the thing that was previously unobservable. Perhaps we should ask, if I see evidence of something, is it not just my beliefs creating the evidence to support my beliefs.

My formula for reality, is the root formula describing the process of turning nothingness into something; and, after removing all unnecessary variables it is a simple equation that works every time and we will see it at work everywhere, all around us, constantly; and, we will understand why many things happen to people and we can often predict what is likely to happen by what they say and do. We will also be able to understand why we have so many limiting "truths" that are commonplace in our reality, due primarily to the efficient use of education, in addition to current messaging targeting other belief systems, to propagate beliefs imposed by the belief systems.

Reality equals the sum of beliefs; and beliefs are nothing more or less than repetitive thoughts and repetitive words. Nothingness plus beliefs equals the literal physical representation of the beliefs.

The energy from beliefs that make up one's reality is amplified the more one repeats the thoughts and/or words. Imagination is the key to start the process where repetition is like the fuel of creation, making it so.

Project management uses conception, planning and implementation, which is basically the same process as the make-believe process described here: conception and thought is the idea, or vision, that starts a project. Planning and word, the expression into reality, is the physical visualization of the project and implementation and manifestation or realization is the action to make it something in this space/time.

Your personal reality is the sum of your beliefs, aka your repetitive thoughts and your repetitive words. Once we realize how this game works, whenever we hear what people are actually saying with their words, we can imagine the reality their words are going to create for them. For example, if they are talking about how horrible they feel all the time and how they are chronically ill and there is nothing they can do, what can their words create given beliefs create everything and repetitive thoughts and words create the beliefs? I would give the person with an arrow sticking out of their back while they are telling people, "They'll fix me up and I'll be fine" – this person has a higher likelihood of being happy in their meatsuit than the chronically ill person who repetitively creates by way of their words, more and continued chronic illness. I should also plant a seed here to hopefully start a thought growing in my beloved family of friends who are talented songwriters and musicians: If you break up with your sex partner and you write a breakup song and you have to sing it over and over again, what will you be helping create every time you sing it? We cannot always impact the collective realities to which we belong, but we can, at the very least, significantly impact our personal reality in a positive way by changing our repetitive thoughts and words, aka, beliefs.

The collective reality of every group of people within which you associate is the product of the beliefs – the repetitive thoughts and repetitive words – of all the people in the collective, up to the largest collective including all people on this planet, yet if something is outside our personal realm of possibility it will not show up for us personally and will show up for the believers within the collective. The creative energy in a collective is multiplied by the number of people in the collective with the same beliefs.

Margaret Mead's famous quote, which I have misquoted to fit the point I'm trying to make, goes like this: Never think a small group of focused dedicated single-minded individuals can't change the world, it's the only thing that ever has. The religionist's son of consciousness started time over with twelve focused followers. In 300 a.d. a group of pagans and christians conspired to create, aka collectively created, a fear-based new religion to control the people of the world and it has worked and continues to work for almost two millennia. Often, there will be one person with a vision that the other members of the collective or team of creator's trust and look to as the leader and direction setter for the team. One skeptic in the collective is all that's needed to delay or even side-track positive desired results – it's best to constantly have each team member state the desired goal out loud with present-tense positive verbiage, along with a knowing confidence of a successful collective outcome.

We need to remember that nothing is here until we create it. Given that nothing is here, there is nothing to discover – the previous assumptions that when we find something that we considered evidence of a discovery, isn't evidence it is created results of previously discussed topics or intended desires of the creative collective effort. Whatever shows up in reality is a created result from the beliefs of the collaboration of the collective consciousness that is responsible. This is the process in action of our beliefs materializing into physicality. This is how nothingness turns into something, before our eyes; and, again, it isn't anything other than the specific created results of beliefs. This is how everything gets here; and it will stay that way as long as a collective keeps believing in it, with repetitive thoughts and words, using any collective, like in a classroom, or even a song.

Let's look at a typical classroom education discipline, like first year college chemistry. Imagine every year in our shared reality on this planet there are hundreds of thousands of creative minds, believing to the point of knowing chemistry into existence by repetitively speaking, listening to and memorizing the fundamentals of the discipline. What better way can one imagine brainwashing a reality into our planetary existence considering the definition and function of beliefs in our reality – from nothingness to a functional set of building blocks to play with on the planet and perpetuate or maintain the creation for many centuries; albeit currently laced with unnecessary limitations that we are fully capable of eliminating with some new ideas about what it so. Education is far more responsible for maintaining creations for multiple generations after an idea's conception, than any other current brainwashing process.

We need not, individually or collectively, to competently understand something to perpetuate it or continue to create it in our reality. Intelligence is not required; however, memory, the ability to express verbally or graphically, including written word, and focus are enough to perpetuate or initiate most any creation. To be educable in our current reality requires a good memory and ability to repetitively demonstrate the subject matter. I would not be classified as educable given my disdain for mundane and undesired repetitive tasks.

Besides education, another great way to brainwash a population is music. Memorable repetitive phrases set to a beat with a melody can become very easy to promote ideas within populations. Music is widely used in commercial brainwashing for product promotion and profit generation, but it can also be used for altruistic brainwashing of positive useful ideas. Music is very useful at creating long term repetitive self-messaging from a very early age. I still remember a song I learned in Sunday school at the family's Nazarene Church before I was old enough for public school: "Jesus loves me, this I know, for the Bible tells me so. Little ones to him belong, we are weak, but He is strong. Yes, Jesus loves me, yes, Jesus loves me…" – over six decades and the message still comes up at random times and whenever I want an example of negative brainwashing for young children. Imagine having catchy songs that empower, and promote loving reactions, and other useful phrases that will act as positive affirmations whenever needed. (Sorry, this has been a deep rabbit hole, allow me to crawl out now.)

Please remember: Reality equals beliefs; and beliefs are nothing more or less than repetitive thoughts and repetitive words. Nothingness plus beliefs equals the literal physical representation of the beliefs into our reality.

From this formula for reality, we can create anything into physicality within our realm of possibility. We can expand our realm of possibility by using the formula to create new beliefs with self-brainwashing techniques like repetitive messaging,

You may be asking, okay, if nothing is here where did all this stuff that appears to be here actually come from? It came from the collective creation consciousness that originally believed it into existence. Often, I imagine, the things came from a collective desire to overcome something perceived as less than desirable. Individuals from the collective may hang out talking about ideas and then they start finding evidence that the idea has merit, but it isn't actually evidence it is actually the start of the creation process leading to more and more creations that are often misinterpreted as discoveries of the way something has always been, but it is actually created by the original beliefs. So often, once something seems to work, people want to figure out how it works, so they set out in another collective to try to explain something the previous collective created, mistakenly thinking that it has always been here or at least it came about for "some" reason; and, it did: it came about because it was created by the beliefs of the original collective and is being perpetuated by its usefulness and social brainwashing including every method from education to songwriting.

This process I just described of collectives trying to explain something that is simply the creation of beliefs – like everything is – this effort to understand, only complicates and often produces parasitic beliefs that serve no constructive purpose, and by existing they distract creative energies from constructive endeavors

Our beliefs create the evidence that supports our beliefs into reality. However reality is for you, this shows you what your beliefs are. There is no evidence without beliefs behind the knowing of it. Knowing something is not possible without believing in it first. The more fervently one knows something the more evidence one will observe supporting the belief. Evidence is nothing more than proof of your beliefs. The illusionary somethingness that you experience in this ESTC game you are currently playing in your meatsuit is nothingness until it is believed into existence.

Consciousness is. In the absence of consciousness, there is absolutely no evidence that any somethingness is here at all. Why would it be? If there is not a source of consciousness, for example, no beings like you or me or anyone, than there is no need of existence and this may explain why science tell us that atoms appear to go into and out of existence all the time – if there is no consciousness to observe it, given that this is all an illusion, why would it appear to be here at all? This is true for any and every "it" that is created and then observed in reality – why would even one illusionary atom be here if there isn't a source of consciousness to both create and then observe it?

Over a quarter century ago, I heard and accepted as truth the following statement: "There is something that I do not know, the knowing of which, will change everything." I still believe this is true for all of us. The main idea behind this book was like that for me.

And now, another message from our sponsors, Your Higher Selves

Post-E2 Brainwashing Commercial FU Grandpa

I hope these repetitive commercial interruptions in the book are not too annoying. I should make a version of the book without the ads so rich people can pay more and avoid the advertisements. Okay, for a million bucks I will intend to get you a copy made without the advertisements. Maybe I should try to add a QR code in the back of this book that would check your credit card first to see if you got a million bucks available, or just Venmo $1M to me – I obviously will sign the million-dollar book and write something nice in it, if you wish.

Before we get back to the proverbial "good stuff" – I would like to try to sell you some ideas by brainwashing you with repetitive messaging – this being the point of this book's existence, please endure this overt attempt to change your mind. Unlike most commercial advertising, or covert attempts to change your mind – I choose to be honest and open about something that likely affects you without you realizing it most of the time. One of my objectives is to make the reader aware that everything you hear or see repeatedly contributes to your physical existence – we will try to make only positive brainwash contributions. We will be right back after this seven-minute advertisement – unless you read it faster than I can say it.

FU, grandpa – Beliefs – 7-minute version

This was originally something I read at spoken word open mics as I was outlining this book. At the time I was watching my 5-year-old granddaughter for about a hundred hours a month, for the previous 40 months (a blessing from covid). I was practicing this spiel at the beginning of her nap time figuring it would quickly bore her to sleep. She actually listened and interjected with her lovely normal attitude. I paraphrased what she said and added foul language that her parents would never condone, to enhance her responses, trying to match her typical attitude and bluntness: (G = granddaughter, D = me)

What are beliefs?

Or maybe a better question is what do beliefs do?

G: "I don't give a shit, grandpa. Talk about something fun, like relationshits or how medical science is full of shit or even how we're all fucking brainwashed. Come on, grandpa, don't bore me. I don't care about beliefs! Aren't we both supposed to have fun — this isn't fun — let's play with my toys instead."

D: *"You need a nap, and I need to practice this for tonight's open mic, so please bear with me for just another few minutes while you fall asleep."*

G: *"Fuck you, grandpa."*

Why should we care what our beliefs are and what they do? Because we can intentionally direct how we perceive reality, how reality shows up for us, by understanding and changing our beliefs to represent the reality we desire to experience.

Allow me to explain this as simply as I can. Our individual beliefs are actually nothing more or less than our personal repetitive thoughts and repetitive words.

Why should we care? Because our perception of reality (both personally and collectively) is created by our beliefs.

G: *"What are you saying, Grandpa? That just sounds fucking nuts."*

D: *"You may be technically right, in which case, dear, please consider this all bullshit. And never believe anything that doesn't feel good and represent what you want more of in your life—you are creating everything with your beliefs whether you think you are or not — so if ever you don't like life, you only have to change what you think and say."*

Allow me to explain why I have come to these conclusions.

Religions tell us we are created in the image of the creator. (Not to support stupid religions; but every now and then certain things have a ring of truth for me. Just like science.)

Science tells us that everything in our reality is made of atoms. And that every atom is 99.999999999999996% empty space.

This means, quite simply and logically, that everything in our reality is nothing more than empty space. That means we can conclude that besides nothing being here (including us) all that we currently believe as real, is in fact illusion. There is nothing here. Quantum mathematicians have expressed that after they add everything up, the sum total of everything is zero — there is nothing actually here!

G: *"What the fuck, Grandpa, how can this be so?"*

D: *"Allow me to explain:"*

The only part of every atom that is not empty space, the 0.000000000000004% that isn't accounted for, is information — exactly the same thing as your thoughts or consciousness.

There is nothing here except remnants of our thoughts.

Einstein tells us "Concerning matter, we have been all wrong. What we have called matter is energy, whose vibration has been so lowered as to be perceptible to the senses. Matter is spirit reduced to the point of visibility. There is no matter." End quote.

G: *"What can this possibly mean, grandpa? It sounds like you're taking me down some fucking rabbit hole, again. Grandpa, do you need to medicate and chill?"*

D: *"No, dear, I'm on a roll, just bear with me."*

This reality is an illusion. And we are created in the image of the creative consciousness; of which, there is only one. That's why we are here. Without this game that you call life (and other games like it) we have no experience of other beings or companionship. Because in actuality, there is no one else.

Just Imagine for a minute that you are the omnipotent creator of the universe. And you are the only one in existence. After eons of what we call time, you are still alone — no one else. You become very lonely. You are, however, all powerful, so you create games to play and imagine stories of imaginary situations where you are not alone. But you were still alone. You cannot be more than the only consciousness; but you, being all powerful, can choose to forget who you are. So, you, the ultimate original gamer, develop a game where you enter the game in a state of amnesia— completely forgetting Who You Are. When you played the game a second time you experienced the image of yourself creating something you had never experienced before: companionship – – there was someone else there — this was a game changer! This illusion of not being alone is the thing that makes life entertaining. You have kept playing the game until it grew to what we currently call reality.

G: *"I still don't buy this shit, grandpa. Do you need your head examined, you old coot?"*

D: *"Maybe, but maybe you should close your eyes and stop wiggling around. Just make believe that you are asleep, and soon you will be."*

There is only one consciousness, playing with itself in the game I call the earth space time continuum.

We are each creating our own personal reality, and together we create our reality with every possible collective (or group of people) up to all people on earth.

Again, whatever we believe (our repeated thoughts and words) manifests in our reality to the level of the fervency with which we know it to be true.

It works so well that if you believe I am full of shit and you know there is no way your thoughts and words (beliefs) create anything, then the reality you create will not show you any evidence that this is the way things work — you are such a powerful creator even if you don't think so. But it is simple, yet often not easy at first, to change our reality in positive ways. I recommend daily rituals to prove to yourself that your repetitive thoughts and words are creative. And eventually controlling your repetitive thoughts and words — thinking and talking only about things that you want more of in your life.

G: *"Is that why we do rituals every morning? It's like you're trying to brainwash me into thinking I'm god or something, grandpa."*

D: *"Please watch your language, young lady — you know we don't use the g-word. But yes, my dear, that is exactly my goal. Now go to sleep."*

Thank you. <whisper>

And now, back to your regular programing entertainment.

THREE -- BELIEFS

Episode 3 Everything Starts with a Belief

The word "beliefs" is traditionally very ambiguous and often thought of as insignificant in regards to our reality, or technically, our illusion of reality, since there isn't anything here, much less, that there isn't anything real to be here. Please allow me to redefine beliefs for you.

An individual's beliefs are nothing more or less than the product of one's repetitive thoughts and repetitive words; and, an individual's beliefs create, with the help of consciousness, everything perceived in reality.

If it's not already obvious, hopefully it will be by the end of the book, each individual has a personal perception of reality (aka a personal pseudo-reality), and every collective of two or more people also experiences a collective reality.

The process of making our personal pseudo-reality is our responsibility because we are the only control there is, it's just that we have experienced so many repetitive thoughts and words all of which become beliefs and thus helps create our personal pseudo-reality. The process of making our planetary reality is a group effort. Every group of conscious humans makes up a collective, from two people to every person currently playing this game of make believe. So, obviously, the sum of all the beliefs of every human on the planet creates constantly what we experience as global reality.

Beliefs are kind of like the building blocks of our reality, if everything here was made of building blocks. A young mind can be thoroughly entertained putting blocks side by side and on top of each other to physicalize the building of simple structures. And then came along LEGO. Smaller in size with various shaped blocks that connect together and keep their shape when the cat walks through the room. As young minds evolve, the intricate results of construction produce amazing results, showing the potential of human imagination.

Imagination, as Google says is "1. the act or power of forming a mental image of something not present to the senses or never before wholly perceived in reality. 2. creative ability."

The smaller block size in the example above significantly increases the resolution potential of the final product. Just like a higher resolution digital camera does to make a clearer image, eventually shrinking it so far you can no longer distinguish one block from another.

Please use your imagination to see beliefs as the building blocks for reality, only let's shrink the blocks down to the size of atoms and also imagine a firmware-like program that connects consciousness to a process of using your beliefs to create everything in perception, exactly the way you believe it to be. Firmware acts as an intermediary between the software, or one's beliefs (aka repetitive thoughts and words) and the code to generate desired results, the beliefs, is like software that creates into physical form, the specific somethingness created out of the nothingness that is.

Beliefs are responsible for everything we experience, for every illusion of physicality, for everything in pseudo-reality, which is everything that we experience while conscious in our meat-suit.

Beliefs create our reality using our repetitive thoughts and words. Our thoughts, words and actions are our creative tools. Thoughts and words form the beliefs that also direct and control our actions.

I believe that beliefs evolve from the first repetitive word or thought that starts the belief growth process. After repetition begins, at some point, we tend to accept the viability of the idea that the thoughts or words seeded. We may, even inadvertently, observe things that support or at least don't distract the belief from growing, potentially expanding our personal realm of possibility. As the data continues to show up in support of the idea, it grows from probable to likely and eventually from likely to certain. At this point the next phase in the evolution of a belief is when it becomes truth, a fact, in our mind. Until this time, it was just a belief, it wasn't real to us, but now it is our reality. The final point of evolution for a belief is when you fervently know it to be so, at which point it must show up as a fact, truth, and real; when you know something, it is unavoidable in your reality.

I think I should actually clarify the above description of the belief evolution process, by adding that when your new belief shows up the first time as being possible, this is actually the belief manifesting into reality for you to observe. Beliefs precede creation which precedes any observation. This is the big problem with the scientific process as it is currently used most of the time. They believe that stuff/things are already here, and we discover them, even though nothing is here, and they've already proved that, so they tend to imagine how something works or where it came from and then see evidence to support their theory, so they believe it even more until eventually the evidence becomes a fact. After a few thousand years of using the results of one belief to create other beliefs we end up thinking a lot of stuff is the way it is and that it cannot change – this is all bullshit – our creative abilities are limited only in our minds – just remember that there is nothing here except for the results of human beliefs. I will get into imposed or brainwashed beliefs in depth later as we discuss belief systems and their current impact on humanity, for now suffice it to say the primary belief systems, which have no function other than to tell us what to accept as truths, each have some useful ideas that I choose to believe, but they all have many potential parasitic beliefs that serve no positive purpose – this applies to all three primary belief systems, which are religion, science and spiritual divinations.

One final thought to this line of thinking related to scientific observations is that the speed of light is also the speed of creation. We cannot observe it any quicker than the speed of light because it isn't there any quicker. Each instant we each create our reality, real time. And again, since there isn't anything here in this illusionary universe, we are technically, as we create our reality, the center of the universe. Yeah, yeah, I know, now I am technically certifiable (please don't tell anyone).

After a message from our sponsors, I'm using my fundamentalist protestant christian childhood brainwashing to make up my potentially useful version of the completely unbelievable Adam and Eve story, either of which are just myths because we have no actual verifiability. My myth fits the model of the make-believe reality that I promote and if it helps to have a model here it is...right after this commercial break.

Post-E3 Brainwashing Commercial Reality Soup

Imagine that your reality is like a big pot of soup, and it is the only thing that you ever get to experience. After the first time that you think a thought or utter a word or phrase, every thought that you have and every word or phrase that you speak instantly goes into your soup. This soup makes up your entire reality. Your every thought and word go into your reality soup.

You don't get to take anything out of the soup, you can only add to it, and do, with your every thought and word or phrase. Your reality soup tastes a little different every day because all of your words and thoughts are constantly being added to the soup and becomes a part of your reality. You can dilute not tasty thoughts and words, by adding more good tasting thoughts and words, but you don't get to just scoop out the bad stuff already there. Minimize the thoughts and words that you don't want more of in your reality while maximizing the delicious thoughts and words of love, appreciation, kindness and everything that you would like in your personal reality.

If you think a thankful thought about your awesome friends and the lovely time you had with them, plop, you just dropped that thought into the soup of your existence. This will add good flavor and nutrition for your life into your reality soup. For the sake of this analogy, this will make your reality taste and smell better – life will be better – than it was before you dropped the good words/thoughts into your reality soup.

Now, say you are going through a divorce, or someone

dies, and life is temporarily filled with thoughts and words that all go into your reality soup. These things usually dominate one's thoughts and words for a longer time than the normal events of life and because of this, the impact on one's reality can last longer than usual – this is why they say it takes time to get over things – it takes time to replenish our reality soup with the usual thoughts and words we have been used to experiencing as our reality – particularly prior to realizing that our thoughts and words create our reality. The feelings of grief and loss can dominate the thoughts and words while we recover which can dominate one's reality via the soup, for longer than usual because of the amount of undesired ingredients put into one's reality soup dominates the flavor until we have time to load in newer positive/good/interesting/uplifting/etc. ingredients (aka thoughts and words). The impact of the undesired event simply needs the flavor to be flushed out with new ingredients until they no longer dominate the flavor of your reality.

This is why I am always saying that it is wise to think and say only things that we want more of in our reality, in our life, in our future. We cannot take anything out of the soup and some things have a very undesirable pungent effect on our soup (reality) as a whole until more desirable ingredients can be added to counter these undesired ingredients and their contribution to our reality.

One easy way to see how our words and thoughts influence our reality is to add specific repetitive words that you enjoy the effect or flavor of. I recommend a daily ritual of positive self-brainwashing including affirmations, gratitude, and intentions; all worded positively with no concepts/words/implications that you do not want more of in your reality. (The actual time it takes to do the ritual can be as little as 5 minutes when you consider most of it, once memorized, can be done while driving, showering, getting dressed, shitting, or about anything else where you don't care if someone hears you say positive things.)

REPETITION

If enough of us start verbalizing positive words and phrases as a part of one's life, I can envision people walking around talking to themselves a lot more after they read this book and/or figure out the value and use of constructive self-talk (aka self-brainwashing, incantations, affirmations, creations). Afterall, you are the most important person you can talk to in your life, and the most useful person too. It can feel kind of embarrassing to speak one's thoughts out loud if we think someone might be listening. We tend to look at people talking to themselves as broken or "not all there", but I have come to realize some of them are just very good at creating their reality albeit potentially ignorant this is what they are doing. If I hear someone saying things out loud to themself that they obviously don't want more of in their life, I am trying to develop a habit of just saying my affirmations out loud to give them a new message and at the same time counter their negativity that might slip into my thoughts (aka my reality soup) as I hear them. Idk if it will help them, but I don't think it can hurt things too much since it's just words. (Haha, I made a joke, like words are not what's really creating our reality when they actually are, along with thoughts, the only things creating our reality – haha, I crack me up sometimes.)

Sorry for the digression, but, regarding your reality soup, here is a method to flush out previous undesired events from our reality soup. Some people have experienced intense and/or long-term negative brainwashing, negatively affecting their reality. This can create undesired ongoing thoughts that we can feel like we have no control over thinking them or getting them to stop repeating in our head, and this creates a very undesirable effect on their reality soup. I have included a process to eliminate these repetitive thoughts later in the book, but it all comes down to directed repetitive self-brainwashing – putting ingredients in the soup to a counter specific dominant flavor, like adding sugar when something is too sour. (Find other references with glossary entry for PCA – positive counter affirmations).

In conclusion, speaking and thinking love, laughter, appreciation, what you like, positive affirmations and PCA's – positive counter affirmations will directly improve the flavor of your reality soup.

FOUR -- NEW CREATION MYTH

Chapter 4 The Story of U

The story of U: A make-believe myth about this make-believe creation that we are currently playing in.

U imagined "Higher You", who imagined the Universe, which then imagined you, again and again and again until here you are now.

List of Character:

U the original gamer, the only inhabitant of ultimate reality, the source of all that is and all that is not, the single consciousness of which all consciousness really is, ultimately.

Self your "Higher Self", the spirit being (or game of games player) from which you come. The spirit source that is you and the only spirit being that knows exactly what you are in your current meatsuit to experience and do this lifetime.

self you in your current meatsuit (also known as your physical body).

Universe the consciousness that is under the illusion of physicality. All that can be experienced by meatsuits, across time. This is why U named it the universe.

Ultimate Reality

U is, was, and forever will be the one and only consciousness. There is no other consciousness. Consciousness is technically a singular concept – there is only one consciousness.

U, being the only consciousness, is the only being in its natural realm which I will call Ultimate Reality. This being is singular, alone, all one. U created games to entertain itself, but U could not escape isolation without a way to fool itself into believing there were others in the game to play with. U is all powerful and all-knowing and ever present (since there is no "time" in ultimate reality). U could not be other than all powerful and all-knowing in ultimate reality. U could create a game where U entered the game in a state of amnesia, without any memory of who it is, who U are.

U chooses to create a game of games within which U can experience the illusion of companionship by isolating memories and forgetting who U are, who it is, repeatedly until a desired number of game players is reached.

The game of games (aka spirit world) – the illusion of companionship

U creates "The Game of Games" where it enters the game in a state of amnesia with no recollection of who it really is. Upon entering the game, U, without memory, becomes Self – a being of ethers still retaining complete control over creation, yet ignorant of this fact and how it works. The life cycle of Self, in The Game of Games starts in full amnesia as a state of total ignorance of who Self is, and progresses to the point of fully remembering who it is – this is what is meant by young souls versus old souls, making the goal or objective of playing the game simply to remember Who It Is? As U chooses to play The Game of Games again and again, the illusion of others is the experience U sought, alleviating the only chronic discomfort of being U, with companionship. (The chronic discomfort of U is from being the only one, being all one, in other words, alone: this is why being alone can be both comfortable – because U are quite used to it – and very uncomfortable – because U are quite familiar with being alone, or all one.)

U enters the Game of Games as a Higher Self in sequence – one after the other. Upon entering the Game of Games, the process of remembering Who It Is (U) begins. Each Self, as it enters the game, starts evolving (remembering Who It Is) while learning (being brainwashed with repetitive thoughts and words) from the Selves that are already in the Game of Games. This creates a difference in the level of how close one is to remembering Who It Is, for every different Self in the Game of Games (aka spirit world). (This is important to remember because when we are here playing in the Earth Space-Time Continuum (ESTC) which is just one (of many) of the games in The Game of Games, any information we get from the ethers can be from any one of the Selves that are in the Game of Games, which means we can get information from a Self that hasn't even played the ESTC, but perhaps has played other games instead, and likely has nothing to do with the ESTC game we are playing here. To get useful information for us individually, from the ethers, one must request information from one's Higher Self. When we calm our mind and receive (via clares) information from the ethers, if we haven't requested information from your Higher Self, it's like we are selecting a random search or even an advertisement and clicking on it, when you likely intend to receive useful information to the self, within the ESTC. If you receive information about the stars or other games in The Game of Games, it has nothing to do with you! While we are conscious in a human meatsuit, our illusion of time is the only measure of how much creative consciousness energy we have to spend – most of us waste a vast majority of our time unconsciously creating, ignorant that we are doing so – imagine focusing a vast majority of our time on our current intention and you can imagine how much more productive our creative efforts will be.

In The Game of Games, the Higher Selves create games within which U can experience companionship or relationships with itself, by also entering into a game within The Game of Games, also in a state of amnesia, where there are really only three things to do. The first thing to do is remember who U are, the second thing is to remember who everyone else in the game is and the third thing to do is reminding other players of the game who they are.

This game, within The Game of Games, allows (U pretending to be) Self, the ability of setting things up before the game is played by agreeing with other players to help create desired experiences and/or choices to make. Much like setting one's itinerary for a vacation – determine where you're going to be when, and planning to meet old friends along the way, while setting up the things you want to experience when you're there. Some of these plans or events that you set up were with only one other Self, some were with just a few other Selves, and some were with large groups, up to every incarnate at a specific event or time.

These things U set up before playing the game within The Game of Games, can be as small as a smile at the right time, or the worst world ruler imaginable creating world holocaust, up to a specie's transition project from a tumultuous time to a time period of peace, plenty and acceptance, without expectations and undesirable discomforts. The players set up many many things to maximize the experience of free choices, just for the experience of it. U see, we should remember this is just a game to help U remember (re-member/re-connect with) who U are.

U chose to pretend to be Self, within The Game of Games. The Self, chose to pretend to be a meatsuit in the Earth space-time continuum (ESTC) game making The Self (aka, the meatsuit's Higher Self). The Self-selects the meatsuit's time period, since there is no time outside the continuum and the Self, each time it plays the game, can enter into the game at any time-period within the ESTC that it chooses.

Each time the Self plays the game, it also brings with it what amounts to a high speed connection to the universal ethereal-net – very similar to the internet of our current game with messages from the ethers including relevant information from one's Higher Self as well as information from many sources that are not one's Higher Self which may or may not have anything to do with you in this "lifetime" or more appropriately "game", since our life is endless and time is an illusion. This connection to the ethereal net is through consciousness in the form of a primary and secondary clair of your predetermination: clairvoyance (seeing images), clairaudience (hearing voices), clairessence (recognizing feelings) and claircognizance (knowing). The Self-selects its primary and secondary clair's, DNA (parents, gender, physical and mental attributes, etcetera) and its itinerary for this next adventure in the earth space-time continuum (ESTC) game.

The earth space-time continuum (ESTC) – an experiential illusion of physicality

Consciousness creates. Consciousness can do nothing else. Consciousness cannot un-create, it can only create anew. Human beings (aka meatsuits) can do nothing but create, while conscious. One thing that's important to realize is that this entire universe is made of atoms and atoms are nothing more than consciousness and empty space. There is nothing real in the universe except consciousness, and consciousness is U.

Inside the Game of Make Believe, your personal reality is whatever you imagine it being or make believe it into being, given your beliefs. Anytime you are in a group of meatsuits, they are also a part of what we call a collective reality. Every collective reality we find ourselves in is made from the beliefs of all the sources of consciousness that are in the collective, from two people to every person on the planet. While in the collective realities we still retain and maintain our personal reality within our personal realm of possibility – we will only experience (see hear taste touch and smell) things we believe to be possible; yet, with an open mind – a willingness to change our mind – we have a free choice to accept, reject or consider new ideas, potentially leading to new beliefs.

Most meatsuits in the ESTC (Earth Space Time Continuum), at this writing, are unconscious to the fact that their consciousness is the source of everything in their reality and it is also the energy behind the illusion we are imagining or currently making believe into what we experience as physicality. There is a connection between every atom being empty space minus the tiniest amount of information to thought and consciousness (remember, there is no matter). So, technically, since consciousness includes all thought, all of this universe is consciousness, and nothing more. To promote the idea of unity consciousness – only one consciousness – I will point out that U are (or, if inclined to use the g-word you're welcome to use it here, god is) consciousness, U are consciousness within the ESTC illusion of separation. There is only one consciousness, get over it, or give me a better reason than having fun with others, for this game of make believe that we are all playing.

In summary, in this version of the creation myth, I have separated human characteristics from non-meatsuit characteristics like gender, physical and mental characteristics. In the game of games, or spirit world as many call it, there is no gender or physical characteristics – no need for sex organs, or any organs, if you don't have a meatsuit. Without meat-suits, we have no gender, physical or mental aspects to associate with our being – we chose our gender, race, ethnicity, physical abilities or disabilities, mental normalness or lack thereof, and every meatsuit feature that we currently have; as well as our major life events and conditions that one has no obvious control over – these have all been pre-selected by us, individually, before jumping into the meatsuit. In the following advertisement there is a version of the creation myth that started out as a young girl as the creator or the universe – this version I originally developed about twenty years before my granddaughter was born.

Post-E4 Brainwashing Commercial Genesis Myth (written for my infant granddaughter)

Below is something I wrote five plus years earlier than the above parable. The names have changed, but the message is the same, pretty much. I wrote it for my granddaughter for her to read when she was old enough.

One.

Once upon a time, a long long time ago -- so long ago that it was actually before you thought of time or needed time as a locator of terrestrial objects as in the three dimensional, here and now, space-time continuum that we are currently choosing to experience. This story I tell you here is about how things started, or might have started, since it was before our time. So, this is not about well documented and provable events but an idea that fits my model of reality, which frankly, I like a lot more than the other major theories on how things got started.

Before I tell you your grandpa's theory on how things started, how they were created, or randomly happened, please let me tell you what I think of the two major competing theories on the start of our universe, our species, and the space-time playground we call earth. The two most predominant belief systems in our reality, at this time, are the Judeo-Christian theories (supported by many religions) and the Newtonian atheism theories (supported by many schools and corporations). Neither Judeo-Christian nor the Newtonian atheists have a viable theory or story from which a loving productive model of reality can pre-evolve and prevail. If the Judeo-Christian ethics believers are right, than jesus will come back (I think on a white horse) and eventually destroy the planet taking all of those who jumped through the right hoops when alive back to an angel made heaven, to a life, as what on earth we would describe as slaves, servants or pets, for an eternity -- which is like a life sentence with no potential way of ending the life sentence since they live forever. I'm sorry that I cannot accept or promote this theory of everything. The other predominant theory of everything in our current environment and time is the Newtonian atheism theory: In this belief system, they don't even understand the concept of "belief system" (even though they are one), which is actually good to utilize spiritual creation tools to unconsciously create physicality. The fervency with which both groups "know" what they think they know, is likely a big reason they're still around and dominate the general calendar for much of humanity on this planet.

One of the biggest reasons I reject the theory of everything that Newtonian atheism promotes is the sureness with which they bring a closed mind to the discussion, often so emphatically that opening the mind to new ideas is not an option, regardless of the consequence or potential value to humanity. In my opinion whatever theory of reality, one accepts as their own should include a viable logical plan to transform the planet into a blissful peaceful environment where we can live without fear, otherwise what is the purpose of the theory or even being here in the first place? The most viable (yet void of love) option for other reasons to be incarnate at this time is perhaps watching us humans blow up this planet (granted, it could be the best fireworks show ever). The other side of this argument is saving the planet from destruction and sending it on a path of love, hopefully with a millennium or more of peace for our species to enjoy the environment/planet.

This all starts with a beginning, or at least this myth about the beginning of something that has always been which makes it beginningless by definition, is going to have a beginning. But again, please forgive me for one more brief delay: Before you were born, before we had first met in these bodies we are using this lifetime, I decided I wanted to tell you something that other people may not know or not tell you if they do know, and it is simply that your grandpa loves you very much and that you are the Creator of the universe and even now you are constantly creating your reality. So please don't ever think you are not important. There is no one more important than you, anywhere.

Please forgive your old grandpa, but I have one more short thing I want to point out before we commence with my creation theory/mythology parable: I want to point out how people in our reality are just creatures of habit or we tend to do things that we are good at and we are used to doing, like we watch movies and shows that entertain us by creating yet another reality to experience other than the one we are currently in. We play games where we pretend to be somewhere else, doing something else. Humans show exceptional talent for creating alternative realities in video games (and movies). It is my hope that by pointing out humans' attraction for movies and games, you will find additional viability in the parable of "O.G. - The Original Gamer"

There is, was and forever will be only one consciousness, only one soul. This one soul, for the sake of this message, in her role as the one and only, which we will call "ultimate reality", is and always has been. This consciousness has been called many things across the ages of the earth space-time continuum -- names like God, Allah, Jehovah, almighty creator, I Am, but for this story we shall call her the "O.G." (for Original Gamer). O.G. is all knowing and all powerful and all alone (all one). For eons of what we would call time O.G. was happy as a clam reveling in the power and knowledge that she is the one and only. She created many different games and stories to entertain herself. She imagined a new way to engage her consciousness and instantly manifested this new way to play. The one and only creator of the universe spends most of Her time creating and playing games, often creating a story within which the games are played. Each game She created helped entertain Her, but none could relieve what was wrong. (A strange thing about finding what is "wrong" with a process -- one first needs to identify how a process produces negative output and how to make these positive outputs. Again, she could not not be the "Only", she is, was, and forever will be ALL ONE, given that there are no others. She might have labeled this problem "ALONE" as an abbreviation for the issue or the feeling identified.) And after even more eons and eons of what we call time, as the one and only She longed for companionship. The OG could not not be the one and only player in all the games.

The O.G. had an idea to create an illusion of companionship. Granted, She could not not be the one and only, all powerful creator of All that is and all the other accolades that distinguish the one and only from the not-one-and-only, but She could create the illusion potential of others by entering a game designed for multiple players putting herself in a state of amnesia, allowing herself to forget Who She Is, forgetting She is the one and only.

I imagine the first time through the game was no big deal. She created the "Game of Games" (GofG) to manifest realities and worlds with endless environments to explore and create (and co-create with herself). She enters the ethereal/spiritual (non-physical) game in a state of amnesia, ignorant of the fact that She is the one and only creator of all that is and all that is not. The goal of the GofG is to remember Who You Are. Again, her first time playing the game was likely, in many ways, similar to many of her previous games because it was done alone. Her experiences in isolation, I imagine, were quite a bit easier to "win" or complete the game (remembering Who She Is) without other people, not to mention all the bad advice from these others, but when there is no hurry to leave or stop playing a game it lends us to consider the argument that life is about the journey, not the destination. So, after remembering Who She Is in the Game of Games she exits and returns to Ultimate Reality where she is the one and only (O.G.).

Later she played the game again. Upon entering the game of games in a state of amnesia, it was the first experience of companionship, of another, of someone else, of not being ALONE (ALL ONE). This was the best gaming decision O.G. ever had, so far, creating the illusion of companionship, community, relationships.

Inside the Game of Games, we created many games and alternate realities in which to play, to experience Who We Are. (Our dreams of fantastical environments where we can fly or do other things unheard of in our current reality could be other games in the GofG.) Eventually, we, as beings in the Game of Games, created the game of reality that we are playing now which I will call the Earth Space-Time Continuum (aka ESTC).

Our perspective of reality which we are experiencing now is entirely from within the ESTC. Within the ESTC we become

DOYLEMOORE

a dumbed down version of ourselves in the GofG. As a being in the GofG we enter the ESTC game as bio-forms (human bodies, or meatsuits), that again are extremely restrictive with only five physical senses and a limited conscious interface with the entity that we "really" are (our Higher Self) in the GofG. In the ESTC we carry our natural creation function with us. Just like the upper layers of the tri-une base reality – layers being Ultimate Reality home of O.G., Game of Games home of our Higher Selves and other players of the GofG, and the lowest layer, vibrationally and systematically is the ESTC where this is being written and read – within the ESTC we are each versions of the one and only creator and therefore have and always will create our personal and co-create each collective reality we experience with other creators, creating with our beliefs (repetitive thoughts and words) using the creative tools designed for these meatsuits: Thought, Word and Action.

This will be discussed in detail later but suffice it to say for now, that yes you are and always have been and always will create your personal reality and co-create your collective realities using your beliefs, but the creation program doesn't recognize time references, negation and functions verbatim. It only works in the present tense -- now, it does not see or understand "not" or other negations lending the conclusion that we need to avoid thinking, saying or doing anything we don't want more of in our reality. Exactly what you say is exactly what you get --" I intend just enough money to pay the bills" produces only enough money to pay the bills, nothing for continuing expenses or savings or anything but the bills. Also, the way you say it may best be as if you already have whatever you intend to create. And finally, don't say shit like "I want" something -- it only leads to a state of "wanting" -- the universe delights in keeping this specific something you want just out of your reach while adding more reasons why you should have it.

There are also factors like the fervency of what one knows to be so will dominate and prioritize creation energies. I think this is how people can earnestly tell you their truth and believe what we know is nonsense and all of our personal realities realize (manifest, materialize) for us.

Okay, back to the story. Where were we? I told you about the O.G. living in her Ultimate Reality making games and creating stories to play in. And how after eons and eons of what we would call time She became very lonely until she created the Game of Games where She enters the game in a state of amnesia, forgetting She is the one and only. The goal of the Game of Games is to remember Who She Is, that She is the one and only, the creator of all that is, and after this She can exit the game any time She chooses and return to Ultimate Reality. If not before, upon entering the GofG the second time, she experienced the wonder of companionship, albeit illusion. (Being alone -- all one -- for so long before the GofG was created, making the game such a good form of entertainment to counter the only truly purposeful annoying feeling in the O.G., loneliness.) In the Game of Games many wonderful games were created to experience this new obsession with relationship, one of which is the current game we are all playing together called the Earth-Space-Time-Continuum (aka ESTC) -- yes, we are all simply playing a game together now. And there is no way to lose the game. Yes, like thousands of video games within ESTC, you can die a million different ways, often over and over for the same reasons before we learn the trick for getting over the obstacles in the way of progress within the game, whatever way we wish to play it. This means there is no "death" to fear, other than the illusions of fear that we choose to believe in.

FIVE --
REINCARNATION AND
PREDETERMINATION

Episode 5 Reincarnation, Predetermination – No Accidents, and Beliefs

Many video games that I have played, or watched my kids or friends play, are made so that when you get to a point in the game that is new, requiring new skills to get through, your player often dies in the process of learning how to get past the next big challenge on the way to completing the game – no big deal. Then you play the game again and when you get to the place you died before, you try something different to advance in the game. And you keep dying in the same place, often for many lives, before learning what is needed to get past the current challenge, or hurdle. This is exactly what we are doing here. The game objectives may be different, but living over and over, often with the same purpose of getting around the next hurdle, completing your life's primary mission or learning from the next challenge, until you get it right, may feel familiar since it is a thing. This is called reincarnation.

(Is it any wonder why this type of video game is so popular? When you think about it, U has been making and playing games like this for fucking ever, so U, as you, have/has been playing the games almost that long – at least the games like ESTC. So, being something we have been doing for fucking ever – making games to play – is it any wonder that we continue doing it in meatsuits while playing the ESTC game?)

The psychology belief system has been hypnotizing patients for over half a century for past life regressions. The patient is asked details about a past life and over the years, many patients have provided significant evidence to make the idea of reincarnation extremely feasible. Someone, while being hypnotized, will detail something verifiable from a past life – maybe, in a past life, they buried something under a tree and when someone looks to find this something it might be found, and has been found for many patients. The fact that it is found just one time fundamentally challenges any scientific argument against reincarnation.

Religion based arguments against reincarnation are null and void in the fear-based fundamentalist christian cults (aka religious belief system). When the Christ centered religions got started three centuries after the time he was believed to be on earth making a fuss and such, the leaders of the new proposed "christian" church gathered books that did not support or hardly ever mentioned reincarnation in order to put together their bible and then they re-wrote any ideas that they didn't like – they made a great effort to not mention reincarnation because the concept doesn't support what they thought was needed to control the population – which after all, was their purpose for starting a religion. They believed that fear-based control tactics were better used to keep people in line, so they came up with this single life, born in sin, jump through our hoops to avoid eternal hellfire and damnation shit that they have now – you gotta admit, it works really well. The problem, for certain religions, with the concept of reincarnation is that it allows for a fearlessness that comes from believing you are already eternal and there isn't anything that can change about this – it's hard to control someone when they say "go ahead and kill me, I'll be back soon; and, by the way, go fuck your stupid fear-based control tactic, you ass holes".

One more side note regarding this christ-based religion distraction. Jesus was an Essene Jew and from what I understand, Essene jews believed in reincarnation and mysticism. And they accidentally left a reincarnation reference in the bible but come along and say it meant something completely different than what Jesus meant when he said it. When Jesus was asked "how can we be like you, Jesus' ', he told them to be born again and again and again; and he meant it quite literally. (And I'm not even going to mention how the bringing Lazarus back from the dead was really his father-in-law testing out a knock-out potion that they gave him on the cross with a sponge so he would appear dead on the first day of something that usually took weeks for someone to die and then showed up to friends afterwards before moving to France where he lived out his life and most likely propagated his lineage with his wife, the Magdalene. Oops, hope they don't read this.)

So, Spirituality doesn't feel left out, I will point out a few things that many current believers of reincarnation are unaware of: "Time" is an illusion. It doesn't exist outside the ESTC, the current game we are playing this lifetime. So, the general belief that our past lives have all come before the current time that we are living in (aka now) and our future lives (in the Game of Games, or spirit world) will all come after the current time in this game that we are playing (here in the ESTC). (This time illusion we experience is a brainwashed belief we acquire from default assumptions we make within the game we are playing and is supported by collective beliefs of most everyone in a meatsuit.) What this means from a reincarnation perspective is that our next life that we choose to live can be at any point on the ESTC timeline. You can choose your next life to be a thousand years ago, or ten thousand years ago. You can also choose your next life to be during a future time. And, the kicker is, you can choose your next life to be at this time, the same time you are living this life, which means, you can actually meet yourSelf living another life at the same time that you are living now. This leads to a possible meeting of yourSelf in two different meatsuits any time two or more of your Higher Self's meatsuits are here playing the ESTC game during the same time. We need to remember that the Higher Selves in the game of games have a life cycle similar to the ESTC and we experience this ESTC life before our future lives and after our past lives. The life cycle for ESTC is from our meatsuit's birth to its death (going home). The life cycle for your Higher Self, playing a game in the Game of Games, starts with amnesia causing ignorance of who you are (like birth), and concludes upon re-membering or fully knowing that we are all the one and only consciousness (going home). If you ever meet yourself in another meatsuit, one of you will have lived the life of the other and may well feel a connection to the other, but the other meatsuit will have no experience of living the other's life in a meatsuit, because it hasn't happened yet in the Higher Self's life cycle. This is a foreign concept to many spiritualists that fully believe in reincarnation. Try to remember two things, first, if you meet someone that you feel close to, or connected to ethereally, but they feel no connection to you, it could actually be you in a past meatsuit; and if you do meet, try to remember to say hi to your Self for U (haha).

This next idea is going to be hard to swallow for many, but there are no accidents. For the most part, everything has been pre-planned and choreographed with all the players or actors knowing (usually unconsciously) just what to do and say to create the experience desired for everyone involved. We all know our roles, we just don't realize this is what we're doing, most of the time. We can crash into another car when there is no way to avoid it; not an accident, it's a preplanned event with someone we don't know here, but we do know in Ethereal-ville (aka, game of games, spirit world, etcetera).

I realize that I'm skating on the thin ice of the philosophical waters between hard determinism and free will. I am not a hard determinist. That would imply a complete absence of free will and make nonsense of everything. I am what they call a soft determinist where there is significant free will, but it's just that we have planned an itinerary for this life and arranged to meet others for specific reasons with pre-planned agendas, all for experience's sake – ours and/or theirs.

There are consequences to our free-will choices, but ...where necessary to meet a pre-incarnation agreement (where things automatically happen), it is our personal choice how to respond, how we react to whatever we are faced with. The choices you make may have far-reaching effects with ethereal consequences, one may be that you will live another life trying to get over this obstacle in your path.

Defining beliefs and what they do

Within the ESTC human beings are consciousness, the

REPETITION

source of the illusion, without inherent limitations. The ESTC would be quite different if only we had been trained from birth to know this and to use this power in a nurturing productive way; but we rarely experience this gift, so far in recorded history. However, unrecorded history may tell us a different story. One story I've heard and come to accept as truth is about when "civilized" humans first encountered a native culture and shortly after meeting set up a footrace for the natives. They put a pile of goodies some distance away from the group of natives and tell them that whoever gets there first will get all the goodies for themselves – all for the first one there. The natives ponder the challenge and surprise the "civilized" by holding hands and walking to the goodies all together, sharing everything. To me, the natives seem far more evolved than the "civilized".

Within two generations of raising our children, realizing who we are and what we are here to do, this planet will transform into a paradise compared to what most beings are experiencing currently. Perhaps you are among those who chose, as part of this incarnation's itinerary, to assist our species to transform this reality away from fear and towards love, creating what one might call heaven on earth – a concept that I believe we are here to implement.

Again, I shall remind the reader that the three creative tools while playing the ESTC game are thought, word, and action. Our beliefs are defined as nothing more or less than our repeated thoughts and repeated words. Everything in this reality is defined by the beliefs of the observer – except it's not really the observer that is observing it, it is the creator creating their own beliefs (along with all other creators present at the time) into this pseudo reality, real time – at, what we have been trained to believe is, the time of observation.

How can we create reality, real time? This is a fascinating concept that discoveries within science have made possible. For me, this belief started evolving multiple decades ago and one of my first arguments for this concept came from the idea that if you were the only human on the planet, the only creative source

67

in the game, and you're on top of a mountain looking out at a view of hundreds of miles of vast scenic beauty, as you are looking out in one direction, what is behind you? I imagined that nothing is behind you. It is not needed in this illusion for you to create anything behind you until you turn around and look at it. But this example doesn't tell us why. Science tells us that we can see nothing real-time because we have to wait for the speed of light to bring it to our eyes. Until we look, nothing is there, when we are the only creative being on the mountain, or anywhere in this pseudo-reality. But as soon as we look, the process of creation is so fast that what we're looking at is visible by the time we created it, before the image reaches our eyes with the speed of light. Real time creation is not only a thing, but also the only thing. (For common creations, things may be a certain way because of group creation of a specific place, but how we receive it personally will be what we make believe.) Science also says that atoms bounce in and out of existence, or from place to place, which would support the premise that the atoms are not used unless a source of consciousness is there to create and observe something.

(I have recently come to believe that the speed of light is actually the speed of creation. We are each, the one consciousness and are creating our reality each moment, so technically, we are the center of our universe. GTFOI.)

The logic of beliefs defining our reality is quite simple to follow. Everything is made of atoms. Atoms are virtually entirely empty space with just a pinch of consciousness defining how they are going to manifest into reality. Consciousness creates, as always, all ways. Within this game, consciousness creates everything from the beliefs of the Self's' meatsuit avatars. Beliefs are nothing more or less than an avatar's repeated thoughts and repeated words. An avatar's beliefs are heavily influenced by the repeated programming or brainwashing experienced in their avatar meatsuit.

The strongest beliefs are those things we fervently know to be so – the universe is hard pressed to show up for us any way otherwise. This upsets some people to hear because it implies, they are also subject to individual interpretation of truth, or facts, and this emotional reaction is indicative of this having to do with the one having the emotional reaction (shadow work). You may be quite attached to the concept of truth and facts being only one way, unchangeable by you and you do not yet observe how everyone, both individually and collectively, not only influences but creates their reality from their beliefs – just listen to what they say and watch how their words show up in their life.

(Shadow work is the process of our emotions spiking when our Higher Self would like us to learn something new about our Self, that we do not currently realize. There are endless things that never strike an emotional chord. The things that get to us, be them positive or negative, good or bad, are always about us personally. Taming our emotions are key to happiness and wholeness. The process usually takes less than a decade to complete, but well worth the effort. Very little can strike an emotional chord once we work though bad programming that our Higher Self feels might hinder our fulfillment of our dharma, or pre-incarnation plans, one's incarnation's purpose or the reason for being here.)

The illusion of reality is completely defined – created – by beliefs. Beliefs, being nothing more or less than repeated thoughts and repeated words, are heavily influenced by the indoctrination or brainwashing experienced up to this point in one's life. This is especially true due to the influence of large groups associated with common belief systems, like religion, spiritual divinations and science – the purpose of which is solely that of telling people what is true and what is not true. We are constantly influenced by belief systems, both what I call primary and secondary belief systems. Primary belief systems are those where the purpose is solely to tell us what to believe in, or what we should know to be true – which is exactly the same thing. Secondary belief systems are every other source of brainwashing we experience, a vast majority of which serve no positive purpose.

Beliefs are consciousness constantly creating reality, real time, instantaneously. We, both individually and collectively, create our beliefs with our repetitive thoughts and repetitive words. The goal is to create a reality we desire with our beliefs by controlling our repetitive thoughts and repetitive words which create our beliefs which in turn create our reality both individually and collectively with every collective we are involved with from two people to every person on the planet. Simply put, think and speak only of things that you want more of in your reality. Think and speak only of things that you want more of in your reality. Think and speak only of things that you want more of in your reality. "I intend to think and speak only of things that I want more of in my reality", you say out loud, all the time, please.

If you are interested in starting the process of consciously creating your own reality, I now recommend a two-week trial of a couple things to start with.

First, turn off as much noise and images going into the mind as possible. All this shit is affecting you, regardless of what you may currently believe. Although I think it is a good idea to throw your television away, I still haven't done so. But I do not have working headphones and I make every effort to avoid listening to talking heads, advertising or anything I do not want more of in my reality. Please, at least for this two-week trial, avoid news, unknown or repetitive podcasts, music with lyrics – unless it's completely positive lyrics with no mention of things that you don't want more of in your reality, advertising of all types, pause the games and turn off everything you possibly can that's going into your mind, from all sources.

Second, say the 7 affirmations, exactly as they are written, out loud at least once a day, every day, for at least two weeks. The key to creating is repetition – say exactly the same thing every time you say them. If you skip a day for any reason, please start the two-week trial over. I am confident you can do this for fourteen consecutive days. And since there are no accidents, you are forgetting to do them for a reason – let them sink in fully by starting over.

The Seven Affirmations

1, My spirit is a field of awareness that connects everything with everything else instantly.

2. My intentions have infinite organizing power.

3. My inner dialogue reflects my inner peace.

4. I know how to go beyond emotional turbulence.

5. I embrace the masculine and the feminine in my own being.

6. Nurturing relationship is the most important thing I can do.

7. I am alert to the opportunity of improbable possibilities.

And when you're done with the two weeks and see that there may be merit to what I'm recommending, please consider adopting the daily ritual that follows this commercial break...

Post-E5 Brainwashing Commercial
Sleep and Dreams

Sleep is needed for the soul not the body. You don't usually see people falling asleep right after physical exertion. Babies tend to sleep more – they aren't used to being in meatsuits yet. Seniors tend to need less sleep because, if they're still living, they are likely on the path they came here to be on. Spiritual masters often sleep very little if at all. In theory, if we are not "on path" we need more sleep and if we are "on path" we need less sleep.

When we sleep, it's like pressing "pause" on the game. There is no time so we can pause it for eons of what we call time before we press "play", to return to the game, awake. During these eons we can play any number of other games with all kinds of scenarios, albeit likely similar in ways associated with what our higher self is wishing to learn/experience. So, some dreams are likely remnants of the other games we play when we are pausing this game, aka sleeping.

SIX -- SELF-BRAINWASHING RITUALS

Episode 6 Daily Ritual – Self Brainwashing Techniques

Before you get too far into saying affirmations and regularly doing a daily ritual, I should tell you that it took me a couple years before I stopped having rather long lapses in my consistency. I would say them for a few weeks, almost every day, and life was good, things were going the way I liked them to go, and I was feeling great most all the time. Then I would forget to say the affirmations for a week or more at a time and things didn't go so well and the shit always eventually hit the fan. This was back when I was working a full-time job in high tech process engineering and raising two teenagers who thought they were adults and seemed to know everything so most input I might have for them was nonsense. I'm sure I was the same way when I was their age, and this was just the proverbial karmic payback that I very likely deserved. In other words, at that time in my life, I had lots of bullshit-adult stuff I had to do, and having high tendency towards procrastination and laziness, and because I was still working I was prescribed 300 - 5mg Dexedrine tablets (aka speed, pep pills, etcetera) every month to assist my ADD and keep a decent job, so, in other words, I was like a good portion of the people in similar situations – too much to do in too little time, and not much of it one would call fun. So, after dealing with life this way, often for weeks or even months, of not saying my affirmations daily, I would finally remember them and start saying them again. Within a couple weeks of regularly saying the affirmations aloud at least once a day, life was good again – no change in what I had to do, it just was a lot nicer to deal with it all. I spent a few years having these relapses and then became very aware if I missed a day or two, because I would feel it. I then added intentions and meditation to the daily ritual and have been quite consistent for twenty years at the ritual. I can't recall the last time I failed to say my affirmations at least once a day, and life has been great, and continually getting better. In other words, don't expect to be perfect, and when in emotional turbulence, say the affirmations out loud and re-start your daily ritual.

Other than what I describe in this book, I do not recommend other types of daily ritual, at least for a few years or until you have firm control of your reality. I know too many people who do things that seem very undesirable in their rituals, from a personal creation perspective. I've heard of people journaling all the undesired things that happened in the day, thinking that if they study them this will somehow make them go away. Reality doesn't work that way. Even if they fervently believe it's doing them good, and are creating evidence for their own confirmation, their life never seems to get better over time. I'm sure you can create a great daily ritual without doing anything that I do, but we need to understand the process of creation and the law of attraction – don't think or say anything that you do not want more of in your life. If you currently have a daily routine or ritual, before you start a new daily ritual like I describe below, it is much easier to see what the new ritual is actually doing if you can discontinue conflicting ritualistic (regular, repeating) messaging prior to starting the new ritual. This can be quite difficult if you have been doing the same routine for a long time. One big problem comes from the idea that we want to list, detail and even speak about things that we don't really want more of in our reality – this will not allow you to stop re-creating, constantly, the things that you do not want more of in your life, your reality. Please remember that you cannot avoid creating a reality that you are already continuously re-creating daily with a previous ritual or anything that you regularly do involving repetitive thoughts and words.

We likely have been trained to detail our failures so we can analyze them and in doing so we think this can eliminate, or at least help get rid of the tendency to fail the same way again. This process does not work! No one can get rid of anything they keep thinking and/or talking about. That is how you keep it – not get rid of it. If you don't want it in your life, you need to stop thinking and talking about it – just shut the fuck up! "Easier said than done", you may say. But your reality is actually always "said than done" – try it – you say it enough and then you start to mean it, and when you mean it, reality starts to show it, and when reality starts to show it, you will begin to know it, and when you fervently know it, reality cannot avoid showing it. Again, often the very best thing we can do about the undesired things that happen in life, is to shut the fuck up – do not speak it and do not think it – "not thinking it" can be harder than not saying it, but techniques to eliminate undesired repetitive thoughts are also detailed within these pages. If you are required to focus on failure, for work or education, try to focus on the solution – how you can do it correctly to succeed; not on what you did wrong; for example, "...I could have done this, that and the other thing and it would have improved the outcome". Sorry for another digression within a digression – I tend to go down rabbit holes, please forgive me if it's annoying.

Suffice it to say, eliminate every distraction you can to test out the usefulness of the following daily ritual. Please try to remember that repetition is the key to creating beliefs, and beliefs are the means by which we direct our creative energies. And, since this reality is all a game, please incorporate a daily GAIM Time in your agenda.

GAIM Time

GAIM Time is what I call my daily ritual. GAIM stands for Gratitude, Affirmations, Intentions and Meditation. After you have everything set up – mostly with Intentions – the whole process can take less than 30 minutes per day. Much of it can be done while doing other things once you memorize the Affirmations.

Gratitude

Gratitude is the newest addition to my daily rituals, but potentially the most valuable. Taking a moment to say out loud what you are grateful for stokes the proverbial ritual fire to improve both intensity and longevity of results. If you are in a situation where you have little time or ability to verbalize it, thinking your gratitude is still productive. Typically, our creative energy – the energy to change our reality – is enhanced with verbalization when the intention is to consciously move reality in a desired direction.

Search your mind for the things to express your true gratitude for. This process, if done regularly as a part of your ritual will allow you to realize other things you're grateful for and how good your life is and even how good it's going to be.

Gratitude for what's on your mind and recent happenings:

Make statements of gratitude for everything on your mind that you are grateful for and include things that have improved in your life since the day before when you last said your statements of gratitude.

Gratitude for the things in your life:

Be grateful for things in your life that many people do not have, like your home and your means of transportation and your ability to survive by doing what you're doing; then, be thankful for what you get to do to survive, to be happy and/or to have fun.

Gratitude for things yet to come:

Expressing your gratitude for things yet to come is a powerful creative expression. Speaking a statement of gratitude for things related to your intentions is a nice way to help speed things along, encouraging us to act on our own behalf.

I can't remember if I picked up the truth that leads me to this conclusion from religion or post-religion enlightenment, but I heard from somewhere that Jesus would pray for things he wanted to receive from the universe, or consciousness, this way – being thankful for things yet to come by thanking the g-word for it, before receiving it. And then, I imagined the effect of this was like the spirit beings in charge of helping us manifest things would hear that this person thinks they already have it, so the spirit beings or angels rush around and get it to them ASAP.

This was a fun way to look at it, but I now believe this is just an exercise to move us from the "believing" to the "knowing", to gaining evidence, that something is so. Again, we must believe something before we will know it or experience any evidence of it – it must be in our realm of possibility.

(I will point out a secret that has kept us from religions overtaking this reality with their goals and objectives: their technique for praying, thankfully, is very unproductive. Saying something like "jesus, please give me this" is a statement that you do not have "this", whatever it is, and the universe delights in continuing you're not having it, just like you said. We will be getting into this later when we talk about grammar requirements for constructive creation.)

So, saying thanks for things not yet received is quite commendable and potentially very useful.

Gratitude – personal example:

My personal gratitude statement for today (the day I'm writing) went something like this. I am so grateful for this beautiful morning and the absence of rain at this moment. I am thankful for my granddaughters and sons. I am thankful for the place I live and the wonderful neighbors and neighborhood where I live. I appreciate my car and my lifestyle and the fact that I live in a continuous state of bliss and happiness. I am so grateful and appreciate all the wonderful people in my life, my music family, my soul family, and all my friends, even those I can't remember – I love them all so much. Especially the young lady that came up to me last night at the second concert greeting me and saying hi and nice to see me again, and I cannot remember her face or name, even after she mentioned her husband's name, who is a drummer I supposedly know, and was with her when we had met before – I love her and am grateful for her, and realize I have already forgot her name and likely won't recognize her next time I see her either. I'm thankful for my mind, even the parts that make me feel like a less than perfect friend, because the part of it that thinks the things that I get to write about is clear and steady. I'm thankful that I am able to complete a first draft in time for a festival this May. I appreciate and am so thankful for the people closest to me that I see and experience regularly – they nurture my happiness. I am also deeply grateful for feeling so good in this resilient functional meatsuit.

Affirmations

Affirmations are the cornerstone to productive ritual and if you have any resistance to taking all the time that it takes to start this complete daily GAIM Time ritual that I'm describing here, I urge you to just say the affirmations, out loud, for fourteen consecutive days to prove to yourself that you do in fact have the power to improve your reality by simply adding only three minutes of positive messaging a day. If you haven't got three minutes a day to improve your life, what are you reading this book for? It's not even three minutes that you have to dedicate to only saying seven affirmations out loud, you can do just about anything else you want to do while saying them: Find the time while sitting on the toilet, waiting at traffic lights or the bus, walking the dog, etcetera. Once you memorize them, you have many other options available to say them out loud including in the shower, while driving or walking – if you don't want others to think you are the crazy person that talks to yourself, stick one of those things in your ear to make you look like your talking on your phone – use emphasis and delays to make it sound like you're having a conversation with someone (that's what I used to do), or find another way to have fun with it.

I have been saying the following seven affirmations, exactly as they are written here, for over twenty-five years with great results. After I first heard them, late last century, I tried to improve them and changed them to suit me. They didn't work anymore. Idk if it is the repetition or the words, but as they are written below, they work! If it ain't broke, don't fix it.

Say the following affirmations, exactly as they are written, OUT LOUD every day for two weeks to prove they work.

Then tell them every day, adding the rest of the GAIM Time ritual to your life as you realize this is the single most useful thing, so far, that someone can do to improve and maintain a happy blissful existence while in a meatsuit.

One last thing, before we start the affirmations: consciousness, in singularity or unity, is the same thing as "spirit", but depending on one's current primary belief system, the two words are interchangeable so if it feels better to you, start the first affirmation with the words "My consciousness..." rather than "My spirit...", but don't change it unless you plan to change it for at least a few months – repetition is the key to effective brainwashing, and positive self-brainwashing is critical to effective improvements in one's reality, in one's life. Again, it's your choice to start the first affirmation with "My spirit..." or "My consciousness...", otherwise please do NOT change even one word, in any way.

The Seven Affirmations

My spirit is a field of awareness that connects everything with everything else instantly.

My intentions have infinite organizing power.

My inner dialogue reflects my inner peace.

I know how to go beyond emotional turbulence.

I embrace the masculine and the feminine in my own being.

Nurturing relationship* is the most important thing I can do.

I am alert to the opportunity of improbable possibilities.

* "relationship" is singular (rather than the plural, "relationships") because we aim to nurture the concept of relationship, not necessarily every relationship, or potential relationship, in our life – sometimes we need to distance or minimize exposure to some people that do not nurture our existence with their existence. I find as I spiritually mature that I'm leaning away from those who will not shut up about

things I really don't want more of, or about things I know they don't really want more of. I give myself permission to be picky. And find myself with more loving friends than I could imagine having twenty years ago.)

Intentions

Forgive me but I'm going to plagiarize myself in this section. I have included portions of the document that I am plagiarizing in some of the ADs between chapters in this book. It is from something that I started writing when my granddaughter was less than two years old that didn't include some of the newest ideas here.

Beliefs create reality. Repetitive thoughts and repetitive words create your beliefs. Intentions, spoken aloud every day, word for word, are the primary means of creating specific things that one desires in one's reality. Repetition is critical for creation – there is too much noise and distraction in most people's reality to affect change without consistent repetition.

Allow me to repeat just to remind and to clarify where everything comes from: beliefs create our personal and collective reality. Beliefs are nothing more or less than our repeated thoughts and repeated words. We have three creative tools (thought, word and deed or action) of which everything in this game of make believe that we are playing, comes from. Our individual realm of possibility is our only limitation to creating anything imaginable. In addition, creation energy is significantly increased due to the fervency with which we know something is possible – a level of great belief or actually "knowing" that something is so, makes it very difficult for our reality to show us otherwise.

Your intentions are the specific things you would like to create at a given time. So, for the most part, intentions come and go. I intend a new sex partner. I intend for this sex partner to go away. I intend another new sex partner. You get my point. For me, the power of intentions became most obvious by the things I intended to manifest, and then once I had the thing

DOYLEMOORE

that I intended I then realized that I didn't want it after all. When writing intentions, it is best to be mindful of the potential consequences of having what you intend.

When I write the intentions for my daily GAIM Time, I like to use three by five cards (color coordinated to categorize long term, short term, planetary, specific project related, etcetera). Then I take pictures with my phone because I tend to misplace the colorful cards within a short time, and I like to look at them every day – this is hopefully something you don't have to deal with. (After nearly two decades of doing personal intentions, I've finally learned to just transcribe it into my phone so I have it available all the time, but I still have my stack of 3x5 cards, too.) As you get started, I recommend a small stack of three by five cards and a rubber band to get GAIM Time started down the right path and keep it with you at least the first few weeks because you may wish to write new intentions at any time.

I recommend starting with only a few general topic intentions regarding health and happiness and the things we intent most of the time, and only one or two specific changes or additions to your life; and, if you wish to include a couple planetary intentions just to save the world I encourage you to do those also -- I'll include them in the example below of what my personal intentions have looked like lately.

Also please remember that with intentions, just like other uses of our creative energies, the one thing we cannot control is any other human -- don't make intentions for other people (unless you are involved with a trusted small collective of people intending to provide a vision or intention with positive, desired, and requested energy, like an Intenders Circle as described in "The Intenders Handbook" by Tony Burroughs).

When writing intentions, avoid using negation like "not" or "no" -- it's as if the words are invisible. Many of my friends are talented musicians that write their own lyrics, and I've noticed situations where the use of "not", likely isn't doing that much damage, or negative creation. For example, "I'm not gonna put up with that shit", may very likely create the same as if you had said "I'm gonna put up with that shit". There may be a backhanded way to create positive by using negation, idk, but try to avoid negation whenever possible to avoid confusion.

Time references are useful to you, but often misunderstood by the creation process. Time is an illusion within this game, but not something understood within the ethers because time is not real. "Never" and "forever" can produce undesired or misunderstood results. ("Never" seems to work like negation and may not be received by the ethers– "I will never stop loving them" is the same as "I will stop loving them".)

Also avoid using "want" and "need" as they create states of "wanting" and "needing" which are usually not what we are looking for, undesirable. This is why we use the words, "I intend" to start each intention.

Avoid the phrase "to be" as this puts it out in the future and as with all creation commands, including our daily intentions, this is typically not effective -- tomorrow never comes. Instead of saying "I intend to be..." use "I intend that I am..." or some other present tense verbiage. Here is where we gently learn to lie, to manifest. Often the most effective way to manifest is to say in the present tense what we desire to have, as if we already have it.

And, finally, avoid saying anything – word, phrase, or even a hint of existence – to anything you do not want more of in your reality.

Intentions usually start with "I intend...". Here are some examples of useful intentions you can use:

I intend love and laughter in my life.

I intend that I am happy and getting happier.

I intend an abundance of all things that I desire and use, including love and money, flowing to me from many directions and sources.

I intend that I feel good in my body.

I intend that I feel great all the time.

I intend that I am in a constant state of happiness and

bliss in a healthy body that feels marvelous to be in.

I intend perfect health, comfort and ease in a healthy body with a clear mind and ambition, helping create a constant state of bliss and happiness in my life.

I intend a place to gather, play, commune and feast with friends and family.

I intend to drink at least four liters of water, write, commune with my Higher Self, physical activity, help something or someone, and GAIM Time each day.

I intend to fervently know my intentions are so.

Planetary/Global Intentions

I intend a progressive tax rate including a 99% tax on all income over one billion dollars per year.

I intend peace on Earth.

Now go ahead and write your first intentions. Be aware of the consequences of getting your intentions. For example, "I intend the new car of my dreams" could have unforeseen financial consequences, where something like "I intend a reliable, comfortable vehicle for the same or less money than I currently spend on transportation". Try to keep the number of intentions to less than six total to start with — please include the two global intentions. Remember no one should intend or create for someone other than oneself, but if doing this with a friend, you can both have the same intention for yourself. The results you get from saying your personal set of intentions, out loud, every day may surprise you.

During GAIM Time, at the end of saying your intentions, please include the following statements, to avoid creating anything that harms and to balance and acknowledge the role consciousness has in the creation process:

"I make all these intentions for the good of myself, the universe and everyone everywhere. So be it and so it is. I express deep gratitude and the greatest thanks to the universe, my Higher Self and the angels and Spirit Guides for already having/

doing/manifesting everything that I intend. THANK YOU."

And just a few paragraphs ago, when finishing up my gratitude statement for the intentions, I also mentioned angels and Spirit Guides. Angels, from what resonates as truth to me, are the spirit beings that hold up our illusion of reality just how we know it to be. By Spirit Guides, I mean the entities in etherealville that are playing the Game of Games as described earlier. (By Higher Self, Jaime /high me/ as I call, she-he-it, I mean the Spirit Guide that is me without the meat-suit – the spirit being that is playing in the Game of Games, as me.) Some of the Spirit Guides are directed by our Higher Self to help us with one thing or another. But there is a life cycle in the life of Spirit Guides (aka everyone's Higher Self), it starts out in complete ignorance of Who It Is and evolves or grows to remember Who It Is and then it can go home unless it wants to continue playing the game just a little longer. (It's not as exciting after you remember Who You Are, so you sign up for harder and harder challenges to experience, but I digress.) Given this life cycle of the Spirit Guides, the information you might get from a young Spirit Guide entity may not be as useful depending on the life cycle of your Higher Self. Old soul, young soul, (yeah yeah, I know, there is only one soul and "age" isn't a thing where there isn't time, but these are common terms that have a useful meaning when trying to understand this stuff) if you're a young soul in a meatsuit, the information you get doesn't much matter, it might even help, but if you're an old soul still trying to catch up in the body with who you are in etherealville, it can make a huge difference and it is not likely useful to take a young soul's Spirit Guide's information or attempts to help. And as for what "angels" are, idk, but if I would guess, and what I believe in my current theory of everything is that angels help hold up the props of this pseudo-reality for our individual and collective beliefs. The angels are the workers to help get things done, and it is worthwhile to consider them in our gratitude's. But you don't have to if it reminds you of god and jesus shit or some other hocus Pokus crap. One more thing to keep in mind, I would request that if you fear something, whatever it is, please face your fears, and they will disappear, but again, I digress – there is nothing at all real to fear, in an illusion.

Intentions are like goals and objectives – they define where we would like the universe to take us, how we want the universe to show up.

Before I move on to meditation, I have a few things to add about intentions that have personally helped me significantly. The first thing is what I've heard called "segment intending" and is done all day long as what we do during the day changes. During transition from one phase of the day to another, be it who, what, or where is changing, simply take a few seconds to intend the next segment of your day by imagining it to be the best (and funnest) it can be. The next thing I say each day with my daily ritual is the phrase "whatever I intend, I intend to have fun along the way to getting what I intend". The last thing I wish to add to this section is yet another thing I learned which is what I've come to call GVGV, which stands for your greatest version of your grandest vision that you can have of something. The GVGV is a good thing to apply to every intention, who you are and especially your visions of both your own and the world's reality,

Meditation

Meditation is like plugging your phone in to recharge it. The best form of meditation for GAIM Time is free from any messaging, unguided, minimizing external brainwashing potential. I recommend a simple 15-minute meditation where you inhale three times, and exhale five times – in your mind, simply count to three and then to five. Meditation can include messaging (typically called "guided" meditation), but I recommend avoiding external messaging of any kind, but rather intend an open channel for information only from your Higher Self. External messaging is any words or repetitive input from your surroundings compared to internal messaging which comes from inside you – be it thoughts, visions, phrases or feelings – these should be remembered (if possible) and then return to a meditation which is absent thought, absent everything. This can be done a few ways: one that I have used successfully is to imagine a clear blue sky free from clouds and when a thought comes in, see it as a cloud in the sky and simply allow the cloud to dissipate and dissolve until it disappears. (If thoughts are consistent, I go back to counting the breaths, 1,2,3 inhale, 1,2,3,4,5 exhale; and if something is particularly bothersome, I will say the 7 Affirmations out loud. If negative thoughts persist, just say the 7 affirmations out loud for the entire 15-minute meditation.)

There are other forms of external message-free, unguided, meditation that I have used over the years that have also worked well. Recently I gained access to a banjo. After watching a video on how to play the thing, it said to learn the picking sequence by practicing it very slowly making sure you pick the strings perfectly, and the speed will come after practice. Just picking the sequence for 15 minutes is a very nice meditation. Exercising, walking, cleaning, etcetera as long as you minimize the external information can be good mediation techniques. I heard something about the time I started consciously meditating, and I may have to try it again someday if I get the chance – some people's only meditation is when they're having sex, either by themself or with others.

The overall goal of meditation is to let the mind do nothing, think nothing and re-charge the ethereal battery.

It is difficult for many people to start and keep a daily ritual going every day. Please say the affirmations out loud, at least. Whenever you do lapse for a few days, weeks, or months, try to make an observation about how life is generally going when the daily ritual is regularly a part of your life and how life is without the ritual – this is all it took for me to realize life was definitely better with a GAIM Time every day.

Daily rituals are a very good way to help focus one's creative energies. Again, all of what we experience is the direct product of our beliefs. The collectives we help create are not always creating things we would necessarily want more of in our reality, but we do not have to contribute our creative energies to any portion of what we experience reality as that we do not wish to be in what we would choose our reality to be. Knowing something is a certain way, is simply and ultimately, your choice, for your personal reality. We are not required to believe that anything specific exists, and we can re-create, create anew, reality into anything that we desire to exist. We cannot un-create anything; but we can create something new any time.

When we start to analyze what this means, humans creating reality with their beliefs, we eventually have to wonder about the very make up of our reality regarding all of the unnecessary, undesired, and ultimately unrequired characteristics of nature/reality. This concept tends to lead to the inevitable conclusion that things are the way they are because humanity has believed them into existence, into reality. So much of this is a byproduct of trying to make sense of something that we experience and assume it to be an observation but isn't an observation – it is our creation. Once we believe something and experiment, often with the best intention to discover how things work, we will think of and then express into reality (speak, write, etcetera) our idea of what's going on, and then find results that verify our assumptions, when we are actually creating the results of the way things work with our beliefs. (Remember, this is a game of make believe that we are playing here in these meatsuits.)

Statistics are virtually always invalid because there is a preference, and/or assumptions, about what the results will be. I was tasked with learning statistics in a high-tech job so I picked up a college textbook for Statistics 101. The first chapter, the first page, stated that there can be no preference to the outcome of an experiment for any statistical analysis to be valid. But, to my knowledge, in twenty years working in process engineering, every experiment that I've ever personally analyzed, or been involved with, had a preference for the desired outcome. In any profit-based environment, there is always a preference, if for no other reason than the experimenter wants to keep their job, or at least get a good review compared to the other experimenters, or engineers. The only experiment that I have even heard about that had no preferred outcome was regarding the first particle accelerator – nobody knew what it would really do. The first time someone "a" turned it on, it produced result "A" with one specific human "observer". Then a different person "b" ran it, and it produced result "B". So, both "a" and "b" got together and ran it a third time, again still not knowing what it would do, and it produced result "C". The lack of consistent result continued until it was eventually torn down and rebuilt with the intention of producing a specific result – which it happily produced to meet the "observer's" expectations or intentions. This is telling me that the "observers" were actually "creators", albeit ignorant of this fact.

A long time ago I started telling people that I am so pissed with Issac Newton – if it weren't for him and this stupid gravity thing, we could all fly (like some of us do in dreams). Sorry I digress, again.

SEVEN -- CREATIVE COMMUNICATION

Pre-E7 Brainwashing Commercial Arguing for Your Limitations

And, now for a short MBBC (Make Believe Brainwashing Commercial) interruption:

"Argue for your limitations, and they are yours."

This is a quote by Richard Bach from the book "Illusions" – I highly recommend the book.

Most of us argue for our limitations regularly and repeatedly.

"I can't do that!", "There's no way that is ever gonna happen", or "This is gonna happen, and it's gonna suck!" "I'm fucking broke all the time." "Nobody loves me." "Nobody really knows what's going on here."

The list of examples of how we argue for our limitations is literally endless. Many of these arguments we have been saying for a long time. They are often embedded in our psyche, something we "know for a fact" and is likely a regular repeating thought, re-creating over and over.

I have a songwriter friend who wrote a song that has a line that says, "nobody really knows what's going on". This is a great thing to say over and over if you like NOT knowing what is going on – if you fervently believe that nobody knows what's really going on, than you won't even see the truth about what's going on when it is discovered and presented to you. Now, don't misunderstand what I'm saying – I am all for ignorance when it comes to not knowing about things that I don't care to have in my reality. I simply think about what I do care to have in my reality and try to repeat that, over and over, with both my thoughts and words.

Some forms of therapy seem potentially unproductive. I believe that every therapist is doing the best they know how, but I question the effectiveness of therapy methods that require a person to dwell on and repeatedly talk about things they do not want more of in their reality. Saying it once to release it, is a good idea, but repeatedly doing so will only make more of the same.

The medical community seems on a similar path, by the way they continuously have you rate your pain and discomfort and provide you with much better drugs the more you claim to feel bad. This technique, although I'm sure is unintentional, is a subtle indirect form of brainwashing that keeps people from the goal of being better.

Please don't misunderstand what I'm saying: I think people do the best they possibly can given what they have been taught is the way to do it, whatever they do — and if not, they are following an internal feeling or belief that they are doing the right thing, or at least, they are doing what they feel they need to do.

I don't believe in malice. I think everyone acts according to what they have experienced so far this lifetime. Most people are loving in nature, but some have been trained (or brainwashed) to live in fear. Some people are horribly abused and come to believe they are justified in doing things that are contrary to a loving environment. There is no intention to harm, it's just the way they're trained to survive, to live, to be.

Episode 7 Effective Grammar for Beliefs

Our thoughts and words are not always saying what we would like them to say. Beliefs are very literal. They don't really care what you say, they will produce exactly what you say, even if it is not what you actually desire to create.

The process to effectively aim reality in the direction of our choosing is simple and easy to understand, yet not usually obvious at first because of syntax and current language habits. Repeated thoughts and repeated words create beliefs and beliefs create everything in this illusionary game of make believe that we are playing here in these meatsuits. Each individual creates both their personal reality and contributes to the collective

REPETITION

realities of every collective to which they belong. Our default contribution to reality is quite ineffective at changing reality due to the fact that creation doesn't understand the concept of time and we are hard pressed to lie by saying and thinking we have something that we do not yet actually have. Whatever we say the universe creates for us literally so we should never use words or descriptions of things we would like to get rid of, because saying the words just creates more of what is said. Creation statements or commands do not understand negation. "I am not a bad boy" is translated as "I am a bad boy".

One of the best ways to look at the grammar and phrase structure of creation is the way a computer programmer writes code to create effective and useful applications that perform how and produce what we would like them to. One thing to realize is that all repetitive thoughts and words in any phrasing we use, is always, in all ways, productive – it's just producing something we didn't really desire if we used the wrong words. So, we might best refine our creation commands by treating them like a computer program, coding them and then testing the program for results.

Common command words to avoid include "want" because it is a statement of not having. If we say, "I want a new car", the universe translates the request to help you "want" a new car so it keeps the new car just out of reach so you can continue to "want" it, it creates a state of wanting, because that is literally what you said. The way I originally heard about words to avoid included three key words to understand, or to avoid misunderstanding, are as follows: you can't have what you "want", If you "need" something, you push it away (to continue "needing" it) and you attract what you "fear" (idk why, other than fear can dominate the thoughts and words when it's on your mind, plus it is illusionary, even within this game that is technically an illusion because there is no matter, and it is the opposite and absence of love – everything "real" in this illusionary game is "love" while "FEAR" is everything that is "not real" within the illusion and F E A R stands for False

93

DOYLEMOORE

Evidence Appearing Real – and always remember, don't confuse or mistake FEAR for consequences that you still believe in).

From my current understanding, the word "intend" is one of the best creative command words that we can use. (This is why the "I" in GAIM Time is for "Intentions".) But even with a constructive creative command word, it is still quite easy to negatively affect an intention with other words. For example, "I intend a new bike that has the features I desire" may be a very productive intention but many of us are inclined (especially at first) to word intentions with words or phrases that can distract the creative energies, like "I intend 'to have' a new bike..." or "I intend 'to get' a new bike..." which are statements that you do NOT have it yet and is likely to act much like a "want" or "need" to make the creative command ineffective. Or, yet another common mistake is using a time element in the intention, like "I intend a new bike by next weekend", or "...by tomorrow", and since tomorrow and next weekend never come so we shouldn't expect getting results from this type of intention until now is actually tomorrow or next weekend – which could take an infinite amount of time. Now is all you have.

If you want to improve your life and learn how to influence your reality, likely many changes should happen to most of what you think and say, given you've likely spent your whole life thinking and talking as if your thoughts and words don't really affect anything; and, you have probably noticed that this is the main point in this book, so I am likely to continue saying this. Controlling our thoughts and words is the only way to control our beliefs and this universe as we experience it has been creating both our personal reality and our collective realities up to and including the state of this entire planetary illusion where we have chosen to play a game of make believe after taking the amnesia pill and jumping through the shoot.

Since beliefs create everything and beliefs are nothing more or less than one's repeated thoughts and repeated words, I highly recommend that if you find yourself saying – speaking aloud – anything that you don't want more of in your reality, just shut the fuck up, or at least say out loud a statement – related or not – that represents a reality that you would like more of.

It seems like many if not all of us can have a negative repeating thought that can produce a negative mood or undesirable feeling. When first dealing with these, the example was about a person that would hear this inner voice say "I'm not good enough. I'm not good enough. I'm not good enough..." repetitively until it put her in a negative mood that was not at all easy to deal with. These repetitive negative thoughts can negatively impact our lives and here is an easy fix that has worked for many people to eliminate many repeating thoughts.

If you find yourself repetitively thinking a thought you don't want more of in your reality, I highly recommend writing the statement down on the top half of a 3x5 card. Please keep these cards handy, so you can easily identify the repeating thoughts. Back when I had negative repeating thoughts, I kept my GIAM Time ritual cards and my undesired thought cards together with a rubber band and it was almost always on my person. If you have an undesired thought that you already have a card for, just put a small check mark above where you wrote it the first time, if it's not exactly the same words but very similar in some way, keep it close to other similar cards for deprogramming later. Upon identifying a repeating undesired thought, on the bottom half of the 3x5 card, write what I call a "positive counter affirmation" or "PCA", a simple positive statement opposite the repeated negative thought, that you would not mind more of in your reality and say it out loud three times, or at least a few more times than you just heard it in your mind – doing this will eliminate the repeating thought from returning indefinitely, within catching it, and countering it aloud with your PCA, a dozen times. (I've never had one last more than 6 times – some go away after just one or two times of catching the repeating thought and saying the positive counter affirmation as many times as you hear it in your head.) Once you have eliminated the negative repeating thought, throw the 3x5 card away – all you need is to read it a few years later and then start it repeating all over again – don't leave shit around to run into that does not represent a reality that you do not desire to be in.

The example that I used over two decades ago when I first taught this technique, was a common repeating thought that some people had: "I'm not good enough. I'm not good enough. I'm not good enough. I'm not good enough…" the mind whispers. The positive counter affirmation (PCA) that eliminated this negative repeating thought by saying it OUT LOUD as many times (plus a few) as they just heard it in their head, is "I am good enough. I am good enough…" The simplest possible PCA is always the place to start.

Many negative repeating thoughts have no easy PCA that reflects a reality you want more of. This can be for a number of reasons and varies greatly from person to person. Just do your best guess and test it for results. Make sure the wording is positive, not saying anything about something you don't want more of and addressing at least a portion of the repeating thought. If the specific repeating thought goes away after using the treatment described above, but another different repeating thought shows up instead, your initial PCA likely addressed only a portion of the original negative repeating thought. Repeat the process, addressing a new aspect of the repeating thought and continue this process – in my experience each time this happens the new repeating thought is less complicated or convoluted than the original negative repeating thought. If you have a repeating thought that doesn't change after twelve times (put a check on the bottom of the 3x5 card each time you use the PCA to count the times you have addressed the negative repeating thought), then simply write a different PCA and try again. After what seemed like years of doing this, I can say that I haven't had a negative repeating thought for at least a couple decades.

Besides "intend" other potentially useful activation words or phrases are "I desire", "I call forth", etcetera up to and including, last but not least, "I command" (if you dare). If you don't get the results, or see some signs supporting your intentions or desires, try a different intention activation – maybe go back to "I intend".

Also, as mentioned before, words and phrases of gratitude may be useful like "I appreciate" and "I am grateful for" but use a present tense statement as if you already have it, for example, "I am so grateful for the perfect reliable vehicle, and a good new home for the car in my driveway".

In summary, make no intentions for a specific person. The one thing we cannot lovingly create is anything that we need any specific person to do – this is a violation of the individuals freewill. Please avoid words that imply you don't actually have what you desire, and it's not a lie to say you have something, once you receive what you intend. Know that what you desire is possible, and that your intentions (and all beliefs, aka repetitive thoughts and words) become your reality, just like they always have.

Some people have found good results in visualization to help bring you what you desire. Vision boards and other popular techniques are potentially useful, just try to avoid images of things you do not want more of in your reality anywhere in the vision. Over a quarter century ago, one of my first ventures down creation lane was a visualization group at a local new age church. I was fortunate enough to meet some spiritually evolved beings, among them was a retired Unity Church minister and a sibling of the author and church leader that started the church and visualization groups. There was a finite group of six people with agreements to spend a few minutes each day holding a specific positive vision, for the other five people, just as we had described it during the group meetings. We met once a week and first went around to say if anything significant happened regarding our vision from last week. Then we would go around the group again and state our vision for the next week – some of us would use the same vision as the previous week – and then socialize for a while so if someone had a question about another individual's vision they could ask for more clarity.

I remember one week, the retired minister told us how

she had been alone for over a decade since her husband had died, and she was thinking she might like to "find a feller", as she put it. She also said that she hadn't had anyone show any interest in her for many years. We all went away for a week, holding each other's visions as usual, and at the next meeting, the lonely heart retired reverend was kind of excited and asked to go first. She said something like "Okay guys, enough is enough. I left the meeting last week and at a stop light on the way home, some guy came up to my window and asked me if I would go out with him. I got home and a neighbor man that I've known for twenty years was on my front porch – he and his late wife used to be friends of ours – he came over to say that he had been thinking he would like to ask me out lately. And the whole week went like this – some guy I hadn't heard from for thirty years called me – this was almost too much at once. I had my first date last night and he was awesome, but now I have to try out a few fellers to pick the best. I am impressed with the effects of group visions. Good work, all; but please, no more guys for now."

If the process of visualizing resonates with you, there is one thing to remember, whether alone or in a group, visualize yourself in the vision. If you want a different car, visualize yourself in the car driving it; don't just hold a vision of the car by itself, it will likely stay that way. (Of course, if in a trustworthy group, be specific about what exactly you would like in a car and ask them to see you driving and getting in and out of it.)

Sharing specifics about what you desire to change in your reality, in general, should be personal unless you know that the other person or people that you talk about it, actually believe that you can obtain what you intend. Their lack of belief may cause a negative effect on the outcome, or at least make it more difficult to obtain. When we do not believe that something would benefit or even believe it is possible, we will only hurt their efforts to get it – worse yet, if we believe it would be bad for them to get it.

Although we should not intend for others without their permission and great care in exactly what we put into the universe on their behalf, that which we put into the universe for another does impact the other. This effect is greatly enhanced in a group of people – it is not just added, the effect from a group is multiplied, possibly exponentially.

That's why gossip is considered black magic or voodoo. It involves a group dynamic to enhance negative energy directed usually at one person or group – repetitive thoughts and words, technically casts a spell. Another good reason to avoid gossip is that you get to experience all the harm you caused, firsthand, when you go home, die, or discard the meatsuit – which are all the same things. We have the ability to not allow the negative creative energies of others, even when directed at us, from affecting us. Once we know who we are and play the game using the "game rules" as described herein, we need only to know we cannot be affected, and we cannot be affected.

The "game rules" or how the universe works to maximize our enjoyment and overall quality of the experience are very simple, yet, because we have been conditioned (aka brainwashed) to believe otherwise since birth, if not conception, we may not believe it until we allow the idea to grow in us. Please believe it when I tell you that your beliefs and learning to change them to make believe your perfect reality, will show you how and why so many things happen to or for people in your life. Believe me when I tell you that you have to believe it before you will see it, or any evidence of it.

EIGHT -- CONSCIOUSNESS

Pre-E8 Brainwashing Commercial
God was

"God is good,
"God is great,
"God is everything that we hate."
(Taco Tapes; hidden song on their second CD)

Episode 8 Consciousness Is

Consciousness is. Without consciousness, nothing is.

The word "god" is no longer a useful term for the creator of the illusionary experience that we call life here in this game of make believe. The g-word, the word I used to call "god", is inaccurately presumed to be external in nature. The concept that the g-word is sitting on a throne up in heaven, no longer serves us. There is no god sitting on a throne up in heaven, period! Why the hell would the g-word need a throne to sit on, given she-he-it hasn't got a meatsuit and doesn't reside in or need to "sit" anywhere.

She-he-it was my preferred pronoun for the single consciousness that I now refer to as the g-word, before the English language redefined pronouns to accommodate an individual's preference which contaminates the human language, potentially creating confusion in things written prior to this century – Imo, definitions of words need to be consistent over time, if at all possible, but always should retain the original intent of the original word. I had an idea over a couple decades ago to write a book called "Holy She-He-It" and write it like a bible for heathens, like me. Please note that if you say, "she-he-it" all together it will sound like a drawn out "shit"; and, my thinking was that "shit" would be a great pronoun moniker for an external "god" or g-word, plus "Holy Shit" would be a good name for upsetting religionists, which I rather enjoyed doing at the time.

When I consider all the accolades I personally place

on the creator or consciousness they are all things I used to associate with the g-word: omnipotent, meaning all powerful; omniscient, meaning all knowing; and omnipresent, meaning present everywhere all the time,

Back to the point I am trying to make, "god" typically is heavily conditioned into many religionists to mean something outside of one's being, separate from the consciousness one uses constantly when that very consciousness we are constantly using is nothing more or less than the one consciousness that created everything, and continues to do so constantly and continuously for everything that is conscious.

One general rule of thumb is, if it has eyes, it is consciousness, aka the g-word, aka "god". I am not limiting consciousness to only life forms with eyes, but idk if plants or other non-eyed life forms are conscious or not – how would I know?

According to Google, consciousness is the state of being awake and aware of one's surroundings. This definition fails to include the scientific fact that nothing, at all, is here – this pseudo reality we experience in our meatsuits is entirely illusionary. The common definitions of both "consciousness" and "illusionary" fail to point out that, absent consciousness, there is absolutely no proof that everything here, or the illusions that appear real here, are here at all. When we consider that there is absolutely nothing really here in the first place, the only thing here at all can only be consciousness.

Consciousness is all that there is. I've come to the recent conclusion that consciousness is not only the only thing through which we can experience anything, but I think it is also that through which we define our reality, or the illusion thereof. We "observe" things in reality with our consciousness and mistakenly think they "were" here before we observed the things, when consciousness also, prior to observation, created (by definition, from thin air) that which we observe before the

REPETITION

speed of light before we observe it, for all intents and purposes, we create instantly, every moment, the product of our beliefs, which are nothing more or less than our repeated thoughts and words.

There is no way to disprove or prove that anything even exists without consciousness to create and then observe that which exists. Why would there be? Since consciousness is both creating and allowing observation of an illusion – given there is absolutely nothing here – why would the illusion be present without something to observe it? Perhaps this is why science says that atoms seem to bounce in and out of reality (assuming they go somewhere else, likely because that fits some previous creation of beliefs, or just an assumption that something is when consciousness isn't – again, no way to prove, either way.) (I tend to believe there is no way to prove anything to anyone except maybe to oneself. Albeit many of us are unaware of this fact, but we are each the ultimate creator of our personal reality and ourselves.)

There is nothing that can be experienced without consciousness.

Absent consciousness, there is not, and no proof that anything even exists.

NINE -- RELEARNING HOW TO COMMUNICATE

Pre-E9 Brainwashing Commercial RelationShits

(This is from a reading I gave at numerous places with mixed reviews.)

How to avoid the Relationshits and the value of forgiving.

You will never find another person that defines love the same way as you do. Even if you have discussed your definition of love and both agree on it, it still won't be the same because everyone defines words and phrases differently as well. I recommend defining love, as you would if you believed the world is a loving place: in my opinion love is best defined as the opposite and absence of FEAR. And FEAR is an acronym for False Evidence Appearing Real. Which makes love everything that is real. Do not mistake fear for consequence. Do not walk across the street without looking until you no longer believe getting hit by a truck will do no damage to you.

If you have ever been hurt in a relationship, stop it! You may not want to realize this, but if you get hurt in relationships, it is all your fault.

Attachment, Buddha tells us, is the source of all suffering. Unhealthy relationships, like we have been trained and brainwashed from birth to think is the way of relationships, are plagued with commitments and expectations, both being nothing more than attachments to an outcome.

Love is unconditional, so one's expectations as well as agreed-upon commitments are not love. We have no control over what another person thinks and does at any time, including when we are in a relationship.

It is difficult, if not impossible, to fix an existing relationship. Don't waste too much time trying, move on as lovingly and kindly as you can.

Start relationships with an agreement to have neither expectations nor commitments. If we have no expectations of another, they cannot hurt us by failing to meet our expectations. This means you cannot feel like they should have done anything specific, and when this is so, everything they do is a gift, not just them doing what you already expected.

Fidelity may be the stupidest concept ever! Even if you find someone that you continue to choose to be with your entire life, why impose on them the absence of loving experiences with others? Even lovebirds that mate for life fuck other lovebirds at every opportunity. This is the only restriction we place on love — if you have two or more cats, dogs, or children, can you only love one of them? Stupid stupid concept!

We are not naturally a coupling species. We are a nesting or tribal species. Prior to the 1400s imposed monogamy was not a thing. It all came about because a pope needed a way to tax the fathers of all the children, so the pope made fucking out of wedlock a sin and required marriage until death. This was a fucked-up system imposed for a fucked-up reason and it completely devastated relationships and the moral right to be open and free with our love and sexuality, which, by the way, love and sexuality may or may not have anything to do with each other.

Well, I probably said enough, but I'll say more anyway. I believe we create reality with our repeating thoughts and repeating words. Say you're in a relationship with someone that breaks your heart because they fucked somebody they shouldn't have, or any reason, and you're hurt and heartbroken and you want to scream to the world what an asshole they were. Say it out loud just one time to release the feeling and move on. (preferably say it to a cat — they won't help continue your undesirable energy)

Try not to repeatedly say anything you don't want more of in your reality. Do not create more grief by thinking and saying your pain to everyone you see—not a good idea. Let's say you're a singer songwriter, and god forbid you write a song and sing it for months or even years re-creating the same reality that caused you the pain in the first place – does not seem wise.

Just one final request, please forgive me. I do not wish to cause pain or discomfort from what I say — that is not the point, but it can be a side effect. I've heard that if we hear something that bothers us there is likely something in it for us, should we choose to accept it. The things not about us personally rarely strike an emotional chord. But this is not the reason to forgive me, or anyone. The reason to forgive is to take your power back from an individual you're giving your power and time to. Forgive others FOR your own benefit, not for them.

One final thought to avoid making a mess of relationshits:

Don't live your life for them, and don't let them live their life for you. Live your life with them for as long as it feels good, and then move on, knowing it lasted the perfect amount of time.

Thank you

Episode 9 Shut the Fuck Up!

You may ask, why is it important to shut the fuck up? Two reasons, but one of the reasons creates the other more destructive reason, making it even more important to shut the fuck up. The first, and most obvious reason is that your repetitive thoughts and words are hard at work creating your reality, with every repetitive thought and word you have. Just so there is no misunderstanding here is how beliefs fit into this equation: one's beliefs create one's reality and one's beliefs are nothing more or less than one's repetitive thoughts and repetitive words. So, obviously, your repetitive thoughts and repetitive words are creating your personal, physical reality.

Now, before I get into the second reason that we should shut the fuck up, I am going to address the feeling we have sometimes when something problematic is bottled up in our mind and we have this urgent need to get it out of our head. The loophole, to do so and get the benefit of shedding the light of day on it which often deflates its intensity, and we can see things in a new light after we get it out of our heads. So, say it once, preferably to your cat or fish or some animal that won't repeat what you're saying or act like they give a shit (some dogs just perpetuate and blow-up things bigger than they need to be, at least in our minds). The problem with saying it to a human, even a well-intentioned human, even one time is if, like a friend might tell another friend and a therapist might write it down in a file and make it permanent in this physicality, I don't personally see either as a positive because of the second reason to just shut the fuck up.

The second reason to shut the fuck up, is the power of collective creation. Everyone has a friend, some of us even do it ourselves, where we tell one or more people all about what happened and how horrible it is, and or how undesirable something is that we obviously do not want more of in our reality. Some of us have the tendency to post online or tell everyone they meet all about the problem thinking that sympathetic replies will somehow help. It never does, except maybe in your mind if you mistakenly continue to believe this process helps something when it is the exact opposite of help, and then only you see it as helpful all the while it is digging you into a deeper hole. Please just shut the fuck up. Sometimes you have so much more power over creating your reality by what you do not say, than by what you do say.

"If you haven't got anything good to say, than don't say anything at all" (aka shut the fuck up). The quote is from my mother. I may have heard that more than anything else she said

REPETITION

to me: "Doyle, if you haven't got anything good to say, don't say anything at all". I don't actually remember her saying it to anyone else but me, go figure. And I imagine that her true self, lacking a lifetime of fundamentalist christian brainwashing, and since now she is in her ethereal condition, having left her meat-suit, she would just tell me to "shut the fuck up, Doyle".) So, if you haven't got anything good to say, shut the fuck up, please.

Many people have an incessant habit or need to explain why something is the way it is. This creates parasitic beliefs. The reason something is the way it is, is the creation of human beliefs, period, get the fuck over it. And shut the fuck up: the thoughts and words we repeat just to explain how the product of our beliefs got here is bullshit, or more specifically unnecessary and anti-productive because it all came from human beliefs, which, again, are repetitive thoughts and words. It doesn't matter how or why something is the way it is; it is enough to know that it is all from human beliefs – why complicate things.

Complication is the opposite of simplification so by its very nature it is an undesirable distraction of our creative energies that could better be used to help create a reality of things we want more of, not what we currently experience. So, maybe we could again STFU (shut the fuck up) about what we no longer want to focus on and by doing so, continue to create.

Focus is also a very important part of getting results from our creative effort, aka our beliefs, aka our repetitive thoughts and repetitive words. If we were to think and speak only of one thing it will show up very quickly, potentially instantaneously; and I'm not sure this is even possible. Keeping the focus of our creative energies on one thing at a time will manifest that one thing faster than if we are focused on two or more things. For most of us, in today's reality, we are constantly juggling hundreds of different things that we have to think and talk about all the time.

We cannot uncreate, but we can spend our words thinking and saying otherwise and it will soon be overwhelmed by our new chosen messaging and become irrelevant until

109

eventually it is nonexistent for us. (Remember the reality soup analogy.) External brainwashing can keep shit around that we don't want in our lives unless we avoid repetitive messaging from advertisements and podcasts and news and everything going into our thoughts. Often, due to our bullshit infested current reality we cannot avoid negative messaging; however, we can use PCA's (positive counter affirmations) to minimize unavoidable, yet undesired negative messaging, like taxes or certain neighbors or politics.

How do you not believe in something that you know for a fact is so? Simple. You brainwash yourself into believing something else. And, again, the process of brainwashing oneself is simply to repeatedly message yourself with words, out loud – saying things out loud uses both thought and word – after we repeat the message enough times, this will change our beliefs and in turn will change our reality. This process is not usually instantaneous, but eventually will start to show evidence of change as the desired message repetition continues; and a new reality is just around the corner. We may need to alter our creative statements as we see the new reality evolving into a full manifestation. But remember, we cannot even go down this path before we shut the fuck up about what it is we do not want more of in our reality that we continuously harp on repeatedly.

Providing your own personal positive self-messaging is highly preferred to the constant external brainwashing that has distorted and seems intent on destroying this awesome playground where we are currently playing a game of make believe. We are currently bombarded by repetitive thoughts and words that we do not want more of in our reality. Every minute you spend listening, watching, talking and playing that doesn't represent what you would like more of in your reality, is a minute of your creative energy that you will never get back. Most of us spend far more time bombarding our brains with information about why something is the way it is, how you feel less than perfect, or someone did something that upset someone, everything that isn't what you desire more of is anti-productive. I highly recommend killing your TV and pulling that stupid thing out of your ear and start becoming comfortable with your own thoughts instead. This in itself may require significant self-directed positive conscious brainwashing but is well worthwhile.

It is commonplace for many of you to talk about undesired things that have happened to yourself or others, often these undesired things have been happening for a long time or may be still happening in your life – it is not going to go away if you keep creating it with your repetitive thoughts and words, so, I would like to lovingly tell you, for your own benefit and the benefit of whoever is listening to you, to please, just shut the fuck up.

To reiterate something I said earlier, sometimes we have something in our head that needs to get out, and we should speak it aloud, just one time. If we need to say something that we do not want more of in our reality, speak it only once, preferably to your plant or cat, as both dogs and people may empathize, which does nothing but create more of the things we do not want in our reality.

Many people have the habit of saying things on their mind, that they do not want more of in their reality, over and over to everyone that will listen to them. If we run into someone doing that, if we would all just say, as kindly and gently as possible, with open arms, "I love you, but please shut the fuck up", perhaps it will make a point.

If you are one of those people and you catch yourself doing just that, ranting emotionally about something that happened or might happen, then just say out loud a counter affirmation or possibly just the Seven Affirmations, and it will help take you off the rant mind-set. We cannot think shit, when we are talking love, out loud – verbal energy overrides mental energy, to change our mind we need only say repeatedly, a new message, aloud.

If in doubt, and nothing good to say, please just shut the

fuck up. Thank you.

And now, a message just for you, from our sponsors to help brainwash you in a positive way.

Post E9 Brainwashing Commercial Thanksgiving 2023

The following is another reading I presented while writing this book:

I'm writing books. The first book of at least two has the working title: A Game of Make Believe. Originally, I was gonna use the subtitle: Get the fuck over it (GTFOI) and shut the fuck up (STFU). But I'm now thinking that's not a good subtitle, even if it might be quite accurate. It is possible my book will piss off everyone in one way or another, because I lay much of the blame for our reality being the way it is on all current belief systems and also on some basic assumptions many have about things that hinder more than help us live free and happy lives.

(First, this is the Get the Fuck Over It part:)

I've been gathering truths like pieces of a puzzle, my whole life, often not realizing why I've gathered the specific information until years later. One of these truths that I learned over 25 years ago, became a cornerstone of my beliefs and started my understanding of what's really going on here in what I mistakenly called reality.

This cornerstone truth was from a book, a conversation with something that I no longer say the name of (except for an occasional expletive deletable). The truth that started me down this path, is that humans are creating their personal and collective realities with their thoughts, words and actions, within this space-time experience that we are all living.

This truth, upon implementing it into my life, started a quarter of a century of every year being better – funner and happier – than the year before. However, I still didn't know exactly how or why this truth made sense in the overall process of our reality— there was something still missing until the final piece of the puzzle landed in my lap a few years ago. Now I know what is really going on here, and I see it in action all the fucking time. So, I figured I better write this shit down because it might be useful for somebody.

In higher mathematics the solution is rarely a number. When there are variables at play the solution is to simplify the formula. This process is often tedious when there's more than a few variables. One tries to eliminate variables that don't really affect the end result until the formula or equation is as easy to understand, with as few variables as possible. That is what I have done with my formula for reality.

Science tells us that everything is made of atoms and atoms are 100% empty space, mathematically, to ten digits of accuracy.

That means that our perception of reality is completely fucked up—reality is more like a pseudo reality or an illusion. There is nothing real in what we call reality, even us.

One of the greatest scientific minds ever, Albert Einstein said, and I quote: "Concerning matter, we have been all wrong. What we have called matter is energy, whose vibration has been so lowered as to be perceptible to the senses. Matter is spirit reduced to (the) point of visibility. There is no matter." End quote.

Another Einstein quote: "Time and space are not conditions in which we live, but modes by which we think. Physical concepts are free creations of the human mind, and are not, however it may seem, determined by the external world."

I've always had great respect for Saint Albert. I feel he is a kindred spirit. Here is one more quote before I get back on track: "Reality is merely an illusion, albeit a very persistent one."

Okay what was I talking about? Oh yeah, simplifying the formula for what we call reality.

First and foremost, there is nothing real in what we call reality— there is nothing here. Quantum mathematicians have concluded some time ago that when they add everything up in reality that the sum total of everything equals zero.

The final piece of the puzzle that I mentioned earlier is a new definition of a common term, yet until now, it has been ambiguous and typically not considered a factor in what we experience in life: Beliefs create every fucking thing in our pseudo-reality; and beliefs are nothing more or less than repeated thoughts and repeated words.

You gotta remember here that there is nothing, NOTHING, here? What makes nothing into something? Not something that humans understand AT ALL! Beliefs might just be involved in making sense of things.

My formula for reality, is simplified to the basics, with all unnecessary variables canceled out and eliminated
Including religion, spiritual divinations and even science.

The equations for reality that I promote are as follows: reality equals the sum of all beliefs. Beliefs equal a person's repeating thoughts and repeating words* (*and other expressions of ideas into this pseudo reality including writing and art). This formula is valid for both an individual and each collective of humans from two people to every person on earth. You, not only create your current and future reality with your beliefs, but you have also created your reality up to this point in your life, using this very process.

REPETITION

My formula, or process, works in every situation for everything that has ever or will ever be in an individual's and in every collective of individuals' reality on this planet if we include the concept of why we are here, and the why is unity consciousness – there is only one consciousness, essentially only one soul, ultimately one being. This is the "why" to this game we are playing here in the earth space time continuum, to experience the illusion of companionship, to no longer be all one, which is also known as, alone.

I believe there is only one consciousness who became an expert at creating illusionary playgrounds as a form of entertainment — the original ultimate gamer. This consciousness was alone and could not be more than one but could enter a game in a state of amnesia creating the illusion of others. One of these games is this earth space time continuum game which we are all playing here. Each of us is the one and only creator of all that is. We are creating our personal and collective realities with our beliefs and our beliefs are nothing more or less than our repeated thoughts and words.

We will never see unexpected data. For example, if we believe everything is the way it is and there is little or nothing, we can do to influence it, than we will not see anything outside of our beliefs, especially what I'm saying, that we are in fact manifesting everything, including the data that supports what we believe, as well as our personal and collective realities.

Our past and future personal beliefs, not only create our reality, but things we don't believe do not exist in our reality, or what I call our personal "realm of possibility"

A good example of the power of one's realm of possibility is from a book I read a long time ago called Hawaii by James Mitchener. In the book is a story about when the first large ships arrived on the islands. Large ships were outside the natives' realm of possibility, and they could not be seen sitting in the bay, only a few hundred yards away. The native population had never seen nor imagined ships this big with massive sails until people from the ships took the natives back to the ships to experience them firsthand. Before a group of natives were taken to the ships, vessels this big were not in the natives' realm of possibility. They didn't exist and were not seen, even though they were huge and obvious once they believed in them.

I highly recommend expanding your realm of possibility, as much as possible, because everything imaginable is possible.

To see evidence that our beliefs create our reality, all we need to do is focus our thoughts and words on things we want more of in our reality and avoid repetitive thoughts and words that we do NOT want more of. I also highly recommend a daily personal brainwashing ritual like the one I call, GAIM Time (spelled G A I M) where G is for gratitude, A is for affirmations, I is for intentions and M is for meditation. So, I recommend brainwashing yourself daily with a consistent message other than the constant brainwashing of one's normal day in modern society, which for the most part does not represent the perfect reality you would desire to live in, or what you want more of in your world.

This is the model of reality that I promote where we are each creators of our reality with our beliefs. I relayed the simplest formula that I could develop that fits all the data, all the time, and once it's believed it will be seen at work everywhere.

(Shut The Fuck Up!)

Many people have an incessant habit or need to explain why something is the way it is. It is the creation of human beliefs, period, get the fuck over it. And shut the fuck up: the thoughts and words we repeat just to explain how a product of our beliefs got here is bullshit, or more specifically unnecessary and anti-productive because it all came from human beliefs, which, again, are repetitive thoughts and words. It doesn't matter how or why something is the way it is; it is enough to know that it is all from human beliefs. And you won't even see or experience it if you don't believe in it.

How do you not believe in something that you fucking know for a fact is so? Simple. You brainwash yourself into believing something else. This is highly preferred to the constant brainwashing that has distorted and seems intent on destroying this awesome playground where we are currently playing a game of make believe.

We are currently bombarded by repetitive thoughts and words that we do not want more of in our reality. Every minute you spend listening, watching, talking and playing that doesn't represent what you would like more of in your reality, is a minute of your creative energy that you will never get back. Most of us spend far more time bombarding our brains with information about why something is the way it is, how you feel less than perfect, or someone did something that upset someone, every fucking thing that isn't what you desire more of is antiproductive. I highly recommend killing your TV and pulling that stupid thing out of your ear and start becoming comfortable with your own thoughts instead. This in itself may require significant self-directed positive conscious brainwashing but is well worthwhile.

It is commonplace for many of you to talk about undesired things that have happened to yourself or others, often these undesired things have been happening for a long time or maybe it is still happening in your life – it is not going to go away if you keep creating it with your repetitive thoughts and words, so, I would like to lovingly tell you, for your own benefit and the benefit of whoever is listening to you, to please, just shut the

DOYLEMOORE

fuck up.

In closing,

I would like to remind you that we are not our bodies, we are eternal beings who chose to play a game in an avatar meatsuit, there is nothing that can go wrong – this life we are living is all a noncompetitive game of make believe, with no losers and no winners. We are here to experience the illusion of companionship and to have fun along the way to this games' three goals: 1) to remember who you are, 2) to remember who everyone else is, and 3) to remind others who they are, which hopefully is what I'm doing with this book, A Game of Make Believe.

And finally, I quote, Saint Albert, one more time.

"We are souls dressed up in sacred biochemical garments and our bodies are the instruments through which our souls play their music."

Please sing a new song, believe into existence, a better personal reality, and a better world. Thank you.

TEN -- DISTRACTIONS

Episode 10 Everyday Brainwashing Influences

Audio video stimulation = repetitive thoughts = ...reality

Given that repetitive thoughts and words create our beliefs which creates our reality, and everything we see or hear instantly becomes a thought, the audio-visual stimulation that the average human experiences at this point in time, is far greater and more influential on the population than at any other time in recorded history.

Imagine humanity's typical audio-visual stimulation for the last two centuries. How many hours of listening to headphones or staring at a cell phone or larger display screen, of any type, did the average human do fifty years ago? Not near as many hours per day as we currently do. Imagine how much unforced audio video stimulation was typical a hundred years ago. Only a hundred years ago there was less than an hour a day average of audio video stimulation and the sales analysis hadn't led to the power of repetition yet – simple marketing is likely responsible for the current brainwashing techniques that are so good that the general population has nothing left. We are told this is not a problem. But we are told this repetitively which results in many people eventually are brainwashed to where they believe this, then their reality will show them this isn't a problem, that we cannot be brainwashed. Before a hundred years ago, humanity had much more control over their individual reality, even though most were quite unaware of this. But today, the amount of brainwashing is very difficult to break through to see what is really going on. So essentially the brainwashing impact on humans is effectively controlling the population by distracting and misdirecting the focus required to create and implement significant positive change for the average person, much less global improvements.

Belief Systems

Consciousness is. Reality, as we perceive it, doesn't exist until it is believed into being by the meat-suits' consciousness that creates it. All that is experienced in this illusionary playground is the product of the creative consciousness inside each source of consciousness within the illusion. In other words, there isn't anything here before it is believed into being, into existence. Without consciousness creating an illusion anew each moment, there is not anything, there is nothing here!

The illusion of physicality requires the leaving of our being inside the nothingness of atoms that make up the experience of the physical into being. Be-leaving (aka believing) is the leaving of our being in the form of consciousness inside each atom in our personal reality – it is the 0.0000000000004% that is not empty space inside each atom that makes up one's reality. The leaving of our being makes the atoms function like other than the nothingness that they are. Our being is consciousness, and atoms are nothing more than 100% empty space and a miniscule sprinkling of consciousness making them function like the illusion of reality that physicality is. So, everything that appears physical requires believing – the leaving of our being – to be physical, otherwise it is only nothingness.

Imagine playing a virtual reality game where you first define the features and characteristics of your avatar, a bi-ped homo-sapiens. Before playing the game, you visit with lots of beings that are also going to be playing the game with you, and you plan an itinerary for your vacation with many friends, some of which will pretend to be something other than a friend while in the game. Then you start playing the game in a state of amnesia, to make believe that it isn't a game at all and that what you are experiencing is actually real. There are no losers in the game, because there is nothing to lose – it's all just a game of make believe where whatever you think and say repeatedly comes into being, into existence, or at least appears that way in the illusionary game you are playing. Consciousness leaves just a hint of being, which we have named be-leaving, inside of every atom that makes up the pseudo-reality within which we play the game. Consciousness is be-leaving, believing, or leaving our being inside the atoms that make up the experience of a reality inside the illusionary physicality within which we are playing the game.

Our being is consciousness – without consciousness we are not and could not exist and would not be anything – consciousness is our being. Believing is the process of leaving consciousness, aka our being, in the atoms that make up the illusion of physicality. Humans are believing this pseudo reality into being. This pseudo-reality that we find ourselves in is the result, or product, of our being, of our believing.

(Just a quick reminder of how this all works: this pseudo-reality that we find ourselves in is made up entirely of atoms. Atoms are 99.999999999996% empty space – 100% to over a dozen digits accuracy – and the 0.0000000000004% that is not empty space is consciousness. This is why it's all a pseudo-reality – because nothing is here except consciousness; and consciousness is everywhere and all that is – there is only one consciousness, one field of awareness that connects everything with everything else, instantly.)

Consciousness is like the central processing unit (CPU) of the early mainframe computers that allow each player, or user of the computer, full access to all the computing power available – each user, depending on what they know, can program, code or create anything they wish to create on the computer, from making a shopping list to writing a book, designing a new supercomputer, designing the integrated circuits that go into the new supercomputer, creating a particle accelerator, making video games, or programming anything that anyone has ever imagined for a computer to create.

The CPU in a mainframe computer allows each user real time access to the full power of the computer, and this appears to all the users that they each have instant answers to basic commands, giving the impression that each user has their own computer, or CPU. They ask for something and the CPU/

computer gives it to them now, without any apparent delay.

The CPU gives each user the impression that they are the only user of the computer that can have a thousand or more users working on it all at once. This can be done because the CPU is so fast at making calculations or fulfilling whatever request users might have for the computer and it does this by giving just a small fraction of CPU time to every user every fraction of a second and this is enough of the computer time to appear to all the users like they have their own computer, but there is only one – it is just much faster and can get more done than we can likely fathom. This is one potential way the single consciousness behind this game we are playing might work to help make us believe we are not alone, when we are all one.

We start this venture in the game of make believe, ignorant of who or what we are. We are indoctrinated, conditioned – we are technically being brainwashed – into believing whatever illusion our parents, caretakers and teachers were brainwashed into believing, much of which hasn't changed since they were brainwashed by their childhood brainwashing experiences. Until we realize we can choose what we believe rather than blindly believing the repetitive messaging we have experienced our whole life, we are creating a reality based on a composite of others' beliefs, one of which is the belief that your beliefs do not influence reality – this is the common blind belief creating an undesired, less than ideal and technically inaccurate, reality in which to play the game.

I am proposing that you avoid blindly believing things that don't feel like your best version of utopia, heaven, paradise, and/or nirvana. Blindly believing is being blind to what you are believing. I imagine that most of you started reading this book blindly believing most everything. As you have hopefully had drilled into your brain by now, our beliefs create our reality, which isn't real at all, and our beliefs are nothing more or less than our repeated thoughts and words and we are all like sponges, absorbing whatever beliefs are repeatedly allowed into our mind, in every way they can get into our mind – it is our choice, our decision, what we allow our beliefs to grow into. Our beliefs have not always been our choice to determine because we have likely been ignorant to how this universe works, how to play this game of make believe that we find ourselves in, and our ignorance has likely included a complete lack of understanding what beliefs are and the importance and value associated of our beliefs and what they do, and have always, all ways, done. What you allow into your thoughts and vocabulary make up your reality and your contribution to all of your collective realities up to and including all creative beings (meatsuits) on the planet. It is your choice and ultimate decision where you direct your creative energies.

Belief systems are any organization that repeats messages to humans, that tells us what is so, what to do, what is truth, or what is real, for any reason. I make a concerted effort to avoid conscious and unconscious beliefs by avoiding association with as many belief systems as possible, and for the belief systems that I must endure, I minimize my exposure to the things that I do not want more of in my reality. Avoiding conscious beliefs is pretty straight forward and easy to address; however, beliefs that are caused by repetitive thoughts that we likely do not realize, that we are unconscious or unaware of, are from messaging in forms including (but not limited to) all images (including pictures, videos, all observations of both unnatural – including man-made – and natural visual stimulation), non-visual or multi-sensory stimulus (including video games, non-video games, and also education – including homework, lectures, mandatory reading and tests),

Again, "belief systems" are any organized group of individuals (a collective) that tell us what is so: be it what is real, what is unreal, what is good and bad, right and wrong, what we should or shouldn't think, do, or act like. They tell us what to think and say, which are the very tools with which everyone's reality is crafted.

Many belief systems have very useful positive beliefs

that may be worth maintaining and incorporating into one's reality. These desired beliefs almost always come with far more parasitic beliefs that serve no positive useful purpose, that we are often simultaneously exposed to and with enough exposure these undesired beliefs become a part of our beliefs and reality also. It is best to avoid parasitic beliefs if possible and may necessitate discontinuing exposure to the things we do not want more of in our reality, including explanations about how or why something is so, often with details about where it came from. The parasitic beliefs about where it came from are belief created concepts to make sense of things that were simply created by beliefs, and trying to find the how, why and where of anything is silly and useless when you realize it all came from beliefs in the first place – the how, why and where's of things may be used to support viability of ideas but are often full of unnecessary bullshit. If you desire to accept a belief as your own, it needs nothing but repetitive thoughts and words for it to grow into fully knowing it into your pseudo reality.

There are two basic types of belief systems: Primary belief systems and secondary belief systems. The primary belief systems' function is to tell people what truth is, what are facts, what is real and how to think about it. It seems to me, from my experience, many of the fundamentalists within each primary belief system get quite upset if you express a lack of belief in what they fervently know to be so. (Emotional reactions are typically because one's shadow trying to get their attention, often in vain.) Secondary belief systems are basically everything that has a purpose behind what they believe.

ELEVEN -- PRIMARY BELIEF SYSTEMS

Pre-E11 Brainwashing Commercial Holy Daze

(The following is a spiel I wrote for the holidays but for some reason I don't think I ever read this anywhere...)

I'm going to redefine the word holiday, talk a lot about nothing, and share with you, your annual holiday gift from the universe.

Holiday is an interesting word. It comes from the term holy day. Holy has a secondary definition of "solemnly dedicated to or set apart for a high purpose". Personally, I am dedicated to be high on purpose, every day. So technically, a holiday is any day that you have the purpose to and are dedicated to being high. Listening to your music gets me high, it is a holiday for me.

Now for nothing at all:

Albert Einstein says, and I quote: "Concerning matter, we have been all wrong. What we have called matter is energy, whose vibration has been so lowered as to be perceptible to the senses. Matter is spirit reduced to (the) point of visibility. There is no matter." End quote.

Another Einstein quote: "Time and space are not conditions in which we live, but modes by which we think. Physical concepts are free creations of the human mind, and are not, however it may seem, determined by the external world."

Here is one last Einstein quote: "Reality is merely an illusion, albeit a very persistent one."

Science tells us that everything is made of atoms and atoms are 100% empty space, mathematically, to more than ten digits of accuracy.

That means that our perception of reality is completely fucked up—reality is more like a pseudo reality or an illusion. There is nothing real in what we call reality, even us.

First and foremost, there is nothing here. Quantum mathematicians have concluded some time ago that when they add everything up in reality that the sum total of everything equals zero.

What can possibly make all this nothingness appear and function like somethingness? What makes nothing into something? This question has not been answered within science, or any other belief system, since it all began. Nor do we seem any closer to finding out as long as we keep ignoring that it is all an illusion, and nothing is here. This is not a process that humans currently appear to understand, AT ALL!

Until we understand the process of turning nothingness into somethingness, we really don't know what the fuck is going on here. And until we understand how to make the somethingness into something that we desire to experience, we have no control over what we experience,

Again, our conscious mind asks, what the fuck is going on here, and why?

The meatsuit that you find yourself in, doesn't exist which means you are not your body; but you are conscious and consciousness. As you go through your day, try to remember that there is nothing, NOTHING, here?

Consciousness is common to all experience. Without consciousness there is no experience, or even perception of reality, much less physical reality – physical reality does not exist, because nothing is fucking real, there is nothing here, according to the greatest minds throughout history.

I believe that our Beliefs are involved in all this. I have developed a theory of reality that explains everything that I plan to share with you next year.

In closing,

Happy fucking holidays. I have a message from the universe, to again present the ultimate present to each of us, of making our own reality soup again this coming year. Our reality is like a soup where every repetitive thought and word is thrown into the soup, as it cooks. I recommend only putting into the soup things you want more of in your reality. Some of us don't realize that certain words and phrases taste awful, or don't produce what we hope. Negation often produces the opposite of what we want more of: "I am 'not' a bad boy", is actually creating as if you had said "I am a bad boy"— "anti-war" produces more war and war tastes horrible. The words want, need and afraid, produce the taste of wanting, needing and fear—all things we don't want in our reality soup. And, as Yoda says, there is no try, there is only do, or not do.

So, this means that exactly what you repeatedly think and say will show up as your reality, for the whole year. This gift is non-returnable. And, again, it happens regardless of what we think and say, which can be a bummer sometimes. Some of us don't want to believe this is happening, which can blind us into not seeing it, like last year.

Episode 11 Primary Belief Systems

There are two basic types of belief systems. Primary belief systems are those organizations whose purpose is primarily to brainwash us for reality's sake, or to tell us what is real and what is unreal, true and untrue. Secondary belief systems are every other organization that brainwashes humanity for any reason.

The primary belief systems require blind faith for the devoted to believe in them. Religion, science and spirituality are the primary belief systems that each would have you believe in their unique flavor of bull shit, so much of it being obviously stupid fucked up ideas that serve no positive function or long-term increased understanding (but instead complicate the simple answer) to what the fuck is going on here in the ESTC. Blind faith is the acceptance of truths without looking to see if it is something one wants more of in their reality. (It is a fallacy to believe that blind faith is accepting something without proof – everything we see "proof" about we are already believing it into existence – we won't see proof until we believe. Since it is our choice to believe that something is true and if we choose to believe in it, we will start to see evidence of it. If we accept a primary belief system as a source of truth and accept everything they identify as true as a personal truth, then we believe whatever shit they fling at us. Humans are, evidently, the most ignorant, naive species in the universe. Just look at everyone that believes in a different primary belief system than you do, and the completely insane shit they believe in – the same thing they are doing, you are doing too. It matters not what one believes, the universe delights in supporting your decision to blindly believe whatever you are repetitively told to think or say. STOP IT! Take back your beliefs by stopping the constant flow of information into your mind through any sensory means including words and images – the beliefs they create, become you. (Again, please choose to create your reality by thinking and saying only what you want more of in your reality.)

Primary belief systems include religion, science and spiritual divinations. Again, the only purpose for existence of a primary belief system is to tell you what is true, aka what to believe in. I have taken many of my truths from each of the three primary belief systems, yet I believe all three primary systems should be abandoned like a sinking ship. I think we are ready for a better primary belief system. Imagine a primary belief system where people are taught that they are already creating their reality with their beliefs and beliefs are simple to understand and have been creating this reality all along. That the time has come for peace, acceptance and abundance for all life on this planet. That we are free to create the very best reality that we can imagine and experience a personal reality that includes happiness and bliss, regardless of how the masses are currently playing the game.

Although I think religion, science and spiritual divinations are all full of shit and not productive for humanity any longer, all three have some useful ideas to include in our beliefs to help us transition to accept a completely new way of believing and can help guide us in creating completely new beliefs. I have come to believe that, if you call forth guidance from your Higher Self, which is the only source of ethereal information that is useful to you, here, while you're in a meatsuit, your Higher Self may provide you with, what I have come to call, a "ring of truth" – the feeling that something is worthwhile to accept as useful and truthful, for you, from certain things you encounter from most any source, including belief systems. Again, the only absolute truth in this game is change – all truths need to be subject to change when concepts are evolving and as you are ready for ever grander, ever greater new truths, and also as your realm of possibilities expands. Allow yourself to define your own truths, to accept those that represent a better reality and/or nurture your happiness and good feelings; while, ignoring most of what they say – it seriously doesn't matter near as much as your focus on the positive things you imagine in a perfect reality. Now let's rip apart the three main Primary Belief Systems and when we're done with that, we will do the same to a couple of the gazillion Secondary Belief Systems available to suck our creative energy for other than a personally chosen reason.

Religion

If you are a religionist of any kind, from a protestant christian fundamentalist to a once a week "confession and you're done" catholic, the one thing you need to realize is there is no god out there anywhere. First of all, there is no "anywhere" out there to be – this reality is all an illusion, where your rule book says "I am" god and we are all the image of god, and since everything is an illusion, with nothing "real" here at all – everything we perceive as reality is nothing but an image of an illusion. Again, there is no god out there, anywhere: Get the fuck over it! The only place you will ever find the creator of the universes, is inside yourself – please, get the fuck over it! We cannot understand how the game was created from inside the game – get the fuck over it! (I'm also sorry about all the "get the fuck over its but...)

One of the helpful things that I learned from religion is the concept of, or belief in, unity consciousness – there is only one "creator" (aka the g-word) – this always had a ring of truth to me, even after evolving beyond believing in the religion. The concept that we are the "image of the creator" is saying much more than how it is defined within the religion – the fact that we are all illusionary by the definition of atomic theory and nothing actually being here, all that is here is technically images of our beliefs to create the illusions. And yes, we are the image of the creator of the game. (It is what we do. We have been creating games or illusionary realities to entertain our Self, for far longer than for-fucking-ever, so is it any wonder that as meatsuits in ESTC, we are creating, playing games, making and watching movies, and imagining ourselves in other realities – these are some of the things that we do really fucking well – both ethereally and pseudo-physically – aka within ESTC.)

(I highly recommend dumping the concept of an external god that religions propose. Replacing the g-word for "consciousness" is a far better concept than an external fear mongering male ruler who has any need for its creation to be anything but conscious on its behalf. Yes, "god" is not a male, or a female, consciousness, when not playing the game of make believe, doesn't have a meatsuit and if you don't have a meatsuit you don't need or have a vagina or a penis, so it has no birth gender, and whatever birth gender one has, was chosen before their birth by their Higher Self. (And please don't make me say get the fuck over it, either.)

Other things I learned from religion are, of course, any altruistic concepts like love your neighbor and be good. Another thing I took away from religion but didn't realize it until much later was how to brainwash a collective (group of people) with repetitive messaging, via preaching, scripture and singalong hymns.

My parents are both no longer with meatsuits, so they won't mind if I tell you how they brainwashed themselves to be good christians. Every morning, they would get up to the radio where a preacher was talking or nasally singers singing the praises of Jesus or something about how wretched we are.

Then, they would actually pray and read the bible. Then during breakfast, they would listen to a different preacher talk. After breakfast they would watch church television shows until noon when my mom would take a secular break with Bob Barker and my mom's favorite game show. After eating lunch while listening to the religious radio, they would return to television brainwashing until nap time. They would continue constant religious brainwashing until evening news where they got their secular brainwashing for the day. Then dinner – oh, I forgot to mention saying grace every meal. Then they would actually, sometimes, watch television shows until ten pm or so and head off to pray and sleep for the night. I came to the conclusion later that it was a lot of work to stay in that unnatural mindset, aka to be a good christian.

Some Parasitic beliefs in religion include the vampirish drinking the blood of Christ and cannibalistic eating of the body of Christ which was a zombie leader walking around after dying – I don't see how that shit in one's reality can be a good thing, Imo.

Maybe the most misinterpreted parasitic christian belief of all is their interpretation of the second coming. I heard a better version in the spiritual belief system that I believe to be the real second coming. I believe the real second coming is when many christ-like old souls will be born on the earth at the same time to help transform the planet into a millennium of peace and plenty – bring it on, Jaime (pronounced /high me/, aka my Higher Self).

Science

Science looks at nature, including human existence, and insists that it is all an "accident", or random chance event after event after event, etcetera indefinitely; yet everything humans have ever made has required design, albeit often lacking what many define as intelligent. Design is not an accident. Actually, this may be too ambiguous – much of what humans have made one could argue was more like stupid, incompetent, ignorant design than intelligent design, but the fact that it would not have been made or created without humans and their use of their consciousness, is what I'm getting at. The problem may well be that, from our perspective inside an illusionary game of make believe, we conclude that we are more intelligent than the intelligence that made the illusion in the first place. These meatsuits that our essence wears in this game of make believe can experience the illusion or physicality only through our meatsuit's five senses and our consciousness. Our five senses together, being the only access to interpret reality by, is like our essence, that which makes us, us, is trapped in a box with five small holes in it and we have to make conclusions about what's really going on from what we get to see through the five holes – we cannot imagine much less comprehend the making, building or creating of nature – it is outside of our ability to comprehend from inside a meatsuit. Science needs to realize there is more to this reality than we can imagine, while at the same time realize whatever we imagine, we create.

The smartest man I ever had the pleasure to work with and be a friend to, was a world leader in material science as it relates to integrated circuitry – he said on a few occasions that if you can't explain something, so a child in third grade can understand it, then you don't know what the fuck you're talking about. (Just in case he's still alive, I should add that he would roll over in his grave before thinking my ideas are viable.) The point being that many people only know what they know because they have had messaging drilled into them, often using verbiage that is not fully understood or comprehended. Unless you know it so well that you can break it all down so a third grader can understand what you're saying, you likely don't really know what the fuck you're talking about – that's okay, it is a byproduct of education and intellect (or the illusion or label of intellect). Intellect and memory are two different things, yet a good memory gets degrees with moderate intellect. Intellect without understanding and discernment is like a restrictive belief system where if you fail to worship the right gods than you will be banished from the circle of intelligence. This is all bull shit, or technically just another way to keep the believers and freethinkers controlled (or fear hell or whatever, the key is to "fear" something). (And I will repeat from my definition of love, which is the absence and opposite of FEAR, which is an acronym for False Evidence Appearing Real – there is nothing "real" to fear, all fears are unreal as there is nothing to fear in the game of make believe that we are playing.)

Many of the best fundamental scientists, all of which are well-intentioned, but education has brainwashed them into believing that their ideas cannot create the data that they intended, but every successful experiment, albeit ignorantly, does just that. Then this manifestation of data is a factual conclusion– the evidence we sought. Then, later, the conclusion is part of another assumption with intention to answer another (likely unnecessary) conclusion which, of course (if the team of scientists have a common intention) will again create a new "discovery" (aka manifestation), and after a few hundred years of this the amount of collective energy "knowing" that these things are so, they must show up as real and viable under any and every reinvestigation of any of the original conclusions. As long as the topic is taught and learned (using repetition) the collective reality of topics taught are perpetuated and continue as facts, regardless of their usefulness or lack thereof. Each of these subordinate observations/creations rely on the original assumptions or the whole house of cards falls down. Now just imagine if Isaac Newton hadn't got hit on the head with an apple and come up with this still misunderstood idea of gravity. Since we can fly in our dreams, we have to assume that other games we are playing do not have this gravity thing holding things down in the same way. (lol) I wonder if we would be able to fly wherever we like, if only we didn't know that we can't. This type of limitation on the viability of new ideas is unnecessary. In summary, as I climb out of another rabbit hole, our observation of "data" is actually our creation of our beliefs real-time into this pseudo-reality.

Imagine a new make-believe science where we know everything is possible with a collective of believers. Where we replace the need to engineer solutions, with the function to imagine-ere our wildest dreams into reality, instead.

But, most of all, science neither understands nor considers the fact that nothing is here in this pseudo-reality, nor does science have any understanding of the process of how to turn nothing into something. (Especially a description that can be explained to a third-grade student and have them understand how to make something out of nothing.)

Some of my ideas may have, potentially, upset some people. I will remind these folks that it wouldn't upset you if your shadow wasn't wanting to change your mind about the very thing you are upset about. And I'm so sorry for upsetting people, but like the omelet makers tell us, you cannot get what you intend, without breaking some eggs.

Some of the things that science believes that I also believe, are important pieces to the puzzle I'm putting together here in this book. (And, yes, we can, and should, just pick and choose whatever feels good to us personally while ignoring all byproducts and what doesn't represent what we want more of in our reality.) (We need no explanations for why we believe it or why it should be believed in – don't should all over yourself.) I've come to realize that my whole life, I have been gathering truths – things that have a "ring of truth" to them, ding – and these truths are like puzzle pieces to a lifelong question that I have had for the ethers, "what the fuck is really going on here?". (Within the last few years, this puzzle has started fitting together into a complete image that does explain how this game is played and where everything comes from and how it gets here.)

Atomic theory is a wonderful creation that quite accurately leads to the obvious conclusion that there is absolutely nothing "real" in this entire game we call reality. I fervently believe the fact that everything in this game is made up of atoms and atoms are 99.9999999999996% empty space. And the thing they don't mention is that is the same as saying every atom is 100% empty space, to over a dozen digit accuracy. Hence, the only viable conclusion we can make is that there is nothing here – this "reality" is actually an illusion, or pseudo-reality – there is nothing fucking here, including us.

You may ask about the 0.0000000000004% of every atom that is not empty space. First of all, this percentage of anything is not physically detectable. And if it exists at all, this infinitesimal portion of the atom is information – the same thing as consciousness, or your thoughts; and, without equipment designed to find something here, I highly doubt they could have concluded that anything is here. Again, there is nothing real in what almost all of us currently fervently know as reality – and the universe always shows us exactly what we fervently know to be so. (Please expand your realm of possibility to include the possibility that science is right, at least about this the conclusion that nothing is here. This game we are playing is quite literally a game of make believe – we make real what we believe to be real, in this illusionary game we are playing.)

The theory about the speed of light, even though I hear the actual speed possibly fluctuates which might lead to many other, likely completely useless, conclusions, is a great reason to make my theory that we create everything real time, every moment, a viable theory. According to science, we can see nothing at the time we look at it – it takes the travel time of the light to reach our eyes, which isn't very much time, but still enough time for the universe to put in place whatever our beliefs are creating in the moment – making, possible, my idea that we are creating everything instantly before the light of it can reach our eyes, or perhaps it's not really the speed of light but it is the speed of creation.

Science currently suffers from the cancerous nature of parasitic beliefs trying to explain virtually every fucking thing when it is all simply the result of our creation – even the data that supports explanation is of human creation and it will show more and more supporting data, the greater the belief becomes, up to the point of fervently knowing which requires the belief

DOYLEMOORE

to show up in the reality of those who fervently know it. I call it a cancerous effect because it grows from assumption to belief to fact, upon which other conclusions grow from assumption to facts, upon which other conclusions grow... I could go on for thousands of years of making assumptions on something we originally believed into existence, but it all came from nothing more than a belief that started with an idea.

Spiritual Divinations

Spirituality was supposed to be the answer to everything, about what the fuck is going on here. The enlightenment from freeing ourselves from the beliefs of both religion and science feels wonderful, until we start to do the same fucking thing science does by creating our beliefs and basing explanations about something our beliefs create to make new "discoveries" in how to find answers from the ethers that are interpretations of information that may or may not have a damn thing to do with the one who receives the information.

Spirituality was a very important evolutionary step in the development of my current idea. I was particularly entertained with the process of allowing the universe to provide me with a specific message from a deck of cards with brief messages on them. I figured the universe knew which card would benefit me and would then arrange the cards so I would pick the card I needed at any given time. I now believe it was a good use of my creative process to believe the information would be useful, and regardless of its actual usefulness, I still saw it as useful. I now think this, or similar processes could still be useful, if we constantly preface the selection of a card with the request that the information is only from our Higher Self. There is a lot of bull shit out there in the ethers: the Game of Games is populated with beings of all levels of ethereal maturity (aka young and old souls), playing all sorts of games (not necessarily the ESTC where we are playing this game) and to just randomly receive an ethereal message we should realize it likely has nothing to do with us, here and now. One sure-fire way to tell if it is not related

138

to you playing this game in the ESTC is if it has anything to do with anything outside of the ESTC – the stars, other planets or species, etcetera. Only accept messages from your Higher Self – the Self that is playing the game in your current meatsuit – that information is useful to you, this lifetime; and, if you don't get anything, it most obviously means that this is your personal decision – it is what you are here to decide, and there is never a wrong choice however there are likely consequences, but again this is for you to decide, not others or the ethers – it is all about you.

I apologize if this strikes an emotional chord in any of my loving friends or readers in the spiritual community, but this would be a perfect lead into the next topic of defining what shadow work actually is, so a third grader can understand it.

It is my goal to help create a temporary and the last primary belief system, one that instills a lack of usefulness for the existing primary belief systems. I think a good primary belief system would include social events including concerts of local singer-songwriters, often with the promotion of a consistent proven daily ritual – modifiable for personal preferences and goals, pleasant positive brainwashing including education options to utilize these new ideas, positive songs everybody can sing along with; and social times focused on including the practice of positive socializing skills where everything said aloud is something desired in the speaker's reality.

Shadow work – the gift of self-discovery

Shadow work is a very simple process with great personal benefits for learning the things about ourselves that our Higher Selves would like us to learn to best be on the path we chose this lifetime. This is often a critical path for which, I imagine, we might end up repeating our requirement to learn in future lifetimes. So, suck it up, this may not be a fun ride.

Shadow work is quite simply how our ethereal guidance shows us by our emotions things about the self, that we need to learn, accept, adjust our path when necessary, and then laugh at triggers that no longer upset us, because we learned what we needed to learn from the emotion. In simple words, everything that pisses you off is always, all ways, telling you that you are doing exactly what the person or situation is doing that pissed you off.

Shadow Work is simply allowing our emotions to tell us about ourselves. Our emotions serve a vital role in our spiritual evolution, beyond simply this lifetime. Like CIM tells it, I am never upset for the reason, I think. Once we're upset, or somehow emotional, we have slipped past the point of self-analyzation — often to the point of attacking but hopefully not "killing the messenger"

If there is someone in your life that upsets you, aka pisses you off, on a regular basis, for what appears like many different reasons, this person is in your life at your request. It may be best to learn about yourself through this person rather than getting rid of them because they piss you off. If you don't learn what you need to learn from them, you will just attract other people who will piss you off, aka activate your shadow response, in ways that may not be so tolerable.

The words or phrases that you call others, with emotion, are describing you. When I'm mad at someone for something, I am likely doing that very thing myself. All the world is but a mirror. These very ideas can be upsetting and should be the first evidence that perhaps this is a truth that you are ready to learn. (Sorry if I've upset you – shadow has a potential to become an emotional rabbit hole – if the idea of the shadow upsets you, perhaps it's telling you to do shadow work.)

The really nice thing after a few years of shadow work is you become very calm and rarely get upset at things because you have learned the things you needed to learn to be calm and happy in your meatsuit. After two decades of shadow work, it's very rare when I get upset, and if I do get the surge of emotions, it's quickly checked, and I know the now familiar process of identifying and accepting a new truth about myself.

There are like a gazillion things around all the time, but very few of them strike an emotional chord in us, aka piss us off. When you think about this shadow work process of telling us the things we need next to learn about the self through virtually all of our emotions, this is both an amazing and effective way for our Higher Self to guide us and at the same time we transform our lives away from undesired emotions towards a drama free life of bliss and happiness – or at least it did for me. (My theory if it doesn't seem to work is that we aren't realizing exactly what the shadow is showing us yet – when we find and accept what we have been doing, that is very much like what pissed us off, there is always a gift in it, and the emotional surge for it goes away when the learning is complete.)

The other side to the shadow work just mentioned, where we discover undesirable things about the self with negative emotions, is where our positive emotions tell us about positive things that we haven't realized about the self. If you see someone doing something and it makes you feel good, there is likely some positive aspect of you that you don't yet realize. The example we used years ago was if you see a person with a child and you notice they are very good with the child, nurturing and instructing, etcetera, and it makes you feel good to watch this, you are likely better at caring for children than you know.

The process of shadow work may be one of the most useful things I learned from the spirituality belief system. I have found truths from each of the three primary belief systems that are currently dominant in our environment. But most of what they would have us believe has nothing to do with our lives and the reality we would desire to be in here in the ESTC – they are riddled with parasitic beliefs. There are other, less popular, primary belief systems that are generally very positive and nurturing, including native american and eastern philosophy-based belief systems, that may provide good examples for a positive belief system, if you really need one.

Before I start with secondary belief systems that attempt to serve a specific purpose for their reason to exist, other than just to tell us what is true and what is not, I will recommend that if you aren't doing anything else with your beliefs, perhaps a Make-Believe primary belief system could provide you with positive, self-directed, brainwashing, for a change. (Please make one up from what you learn in this book please.)

TWELVE -- SECONDARY BELIEF SYSTEMS

Pre-E12.1 Brainwashing Commercial
Process Engineering's "Big Red X"

How to fix a process problem: The Big red X.

For many years, while I was under the illusion that statistically valid experiments were a thing, I became quite familiar with designing experiments to tell me something about a normal population. There is a need for a normal population, be it natural or normalized, to be able to predict the likelihood by calculating the probability of potential outcomes. This was usually done with two way or three-way comparative analysis of an experiment's results to determine distribution including modalities along with the usual predictive indicators for center and variation, given there are no distribution related abnormalities, of both a control and however many other variables are in the experiment. Simple stuff, just playing the game.

I was not an easy person to convince that the solution that they wanted to implement was the real solution to the problem. It became a concern that the experiments were not being designed properly, or at the time, that was what I presumed. They would have data showing a statistically significant improvement but the number of fliers that could switch the results good to bad just from omission or inclusion of the flier data, and it should be obvious that it doesn't make a lot of sense to use the experiment data if that's the case. I was labeled a skeptic. But my laziness had driven me to automation and process efficiency, so they let me keep working there.

In my later days of working in a large integrated circuit fabrication facility, I had pretty good results with what I did, but I never bothered getting my college degree which made it more difficult to get certain job titles but for a few years I worked on a process that was only going to be needed for a few more years and it didn't require as much engineering staff because there was no longer a concerted effort to continuously make process improvements – which I was just about to prove wasn't usually making any actual improvements. They left me in charge of fabrication engineering by way of the approval link for all process changes including all experiments. So, I didn't approve any changes whatsoever for over two years and in doing so our productivity, or yield as they called it, was the best of any facility in their history, at that time. Looking back, I now believe that my strong beliefs that all the changes made to make engineering departments look productive were not productive, however management likes data and graphs showing that the engineering department was doing something, albeit mostly much to do about nothing. The engineering department would have been more productive to spend almost all their time identifying the single biggest influence on the product, rather than every statistical signal that was not where the process improvement could be found

Somewhere between year 7 and 11 of my twenty-year career in high tech, I went to a week-long training for process engineering statistics, taught by an old guy named Jake Shredne from somewhere in Europe or the Middle east. He had a few nifty tricks to get statistically significant signals from only 6 samples in a two-way experiment, as long as the populations are not overlapping – this is what most of my colleagues took away and used, likely for the rest of their careers. But the thing I took away from the training was the concept of "the big red X". which says that, unless you want to go back later and undo most, if not all, of the recent changes made in hopes of making things better, you need to identify and fix the most significant variable in the process. The most significant variable, the first thing that needs to be fixed, is not always easy to find, but if we don't find and fix it first, we likely won't make things better in the long run.

I have been blessed with being able to find the big red X in many situations. Idk how, but usually after pondering a problem intuition brings an idea, and the idea often leads to supporting details that can add confidence that I'm on the right

DOYLEMOORE

path. Since learning this process over thirty-five years ago, I used it successfully in my high tech career for many years, during which I stumbled on the big red X for the human healthcare process and applied the fix to my life and any of my friends that would consider the fix and everyone that applied it fully saw the same overwhelming improvements in their health just like I did. Having grown up in a time of plenty and experiencing the changes over the last forty plus years in the economic make-up of a typical American family, the cause and solution became obvious based on my experience. I will, in later chapters, share both these big red X solutions that will have a huge social/economic impact, upon implementation. The healthcare solution is free and individual – you can do it for yourself without spending money – you will likely save money and feel much better upon implementing this fix. The social problem is going to require a collective effort that we can do together, we just need to focus on the solution, not the problem and it will happen.

Focusing on problems only makes more problems. This is the big reason I'm always telling people to "shut the fuck up". Thinking about what's wrong, will neither create what's right, nor even something better, it can only help produce more of what's wrong. We need to think and express (say, write, draw, etc.) what we desire, to help grow what we are after. (And, because of this, I try to minimize my discussion of a "problem" without also expressing a "solution".)

Before I tell you what the big red X is for a couple large boulders on our path that we will be better off without, I would like to tell you what the biggest and most effective conspiracy is ever popularized within our current rhetoric. The biggest conspiracy ever conspired to negatively influence what and how we think about things, has been the conspiracy to downplay and belittle conspiracy theories. By definition, if a group of corporate employees sit and plan ways to make more money at the cost of customers and/or the general public, it is a conspiracy. A conspiracy is a secret plan by a group to do something wrong or harmful. (Technically conspiracy refers to things "unlawful or harmful", but when one of the many conspiracies along the path of conspiracies we aren't allowed to consider because we are a no good conspiracy theorist if we even think about it, was a conspiracy to buy both major political parties and change the laws to allow price gouging and monopolies, not to mention many other things most people would consider "wrong", and in doing so, made it "legal" to charge two to three times what thing cost only a few years back.) "Our fine colleague from the packaging department has a great idea to increase profits that most customers will never even realize – we simply use the same package and put less in it – they'll likely never notice."

Perhaps the opposite of conspire should be inspire. So, perhaps we need a new word for open collaboration and planning to improve things. Rather than a conspiracy to conspire perhaps we could have an "inspiracy" to inspire. Let me define "inspiracy": to openly discuss and plan the implementation of positive, loving ideas that help humanity while nurturing life on the planet – or something like that.

Pre-E12.2 Brainwashing Commercial
More brainwashing from the past

To introduce the following advertisement, I should maybe try to tell you when and why it was written and why it wasn't completed (and maybe what I didn't know then that I know now), but I probably won't.

From 2019

Two decades of near indentured servitude to the likes of high-tech giants still causing traffic jams and start-up companies that no longer exist provided me with an education and skills in process engineering, including an understanding of the concept of "the big red X" which is exactly what we need to change/fix/improve most any process including human health, world peace and general global repair. The big red X is the concept of finding and fixing the single biggest problem within a process and watching much, if not all, of the other problems simply go away as secondary or parasitic signals also caused by the big red X (quite repeatedly provable by trying it out). I watched and used the big red X concept for many process problems in my workplace at the time, always with excellent results. There are a couple other big red X's that I have identified and should prove to be very helpful within the related processes.

The first process that I applied the "big red x system" to is the human health process. There is no sure-fire way to make what I'm about to say sound any less crazy than how it sounds, but I shall try. When I was in elementary school, I had stomach aches that would send me home sick, mid-afternoon maybe a couple times a week, at its worst. The doctor, whom I thought a quack at ten years old, was actually a wise old osteopath with good advice, that I could not believe to be true, wishing he would give me a pill to cure my ailments, so eventually he did, but it didn't cure my bad stomach it only made things a little better if at all. I continued down this path of an upset stomach which got labeled "pre-ulcer syndrome" for another 25 years with additional health problems including asthma, acid reflux, and a myriad of chronic illness indications. By the time I stumbled onto the cure for most ailments modern humans are bothered by me was having an elective surgery to cure my snoring, during the recovery of which, I was faced with the worst sore throat of my life and the only thing I could find to relieve the pain was a constant flow of ice water across my recovering uvula. Needless to say, being a wimp when it comes to pain in any way, I kept a constant flow of ice water easing pain and having the side effect of rehydrating my body for the first time in over a quarter of a century. During this two-week surgery recovery, I permanently cured my asthma, IBS, and all stomach pain including chronic constipation, with water.

A few months later, I came across the book "Your Bodies

Many Cries for Water" by Dr. F. Batmanghelidj where he details what is going on in human health regarding water. Basically, in nature there is nothing to drink but water. In our current society, many people drink very little if any pure water. (Pure water for this discussion refers to water without anything added to it for flavor or attempts to add other chemicals to the body.) Any liquid except pure water must be processed through the kidney (likely with help from your liver) to filter the water (for the body) out of the non-water (aka "poison") that we are making ourselves ill with.

Dr Batman* tried to get medical science in the USA to research the data collected for seven years as a doctor and political prisoner in the middle east, treating many diseases successfully with water. But all medical research done in universities in the USA must be sponsored by a pharmaceutical company. There is no profit potential in finding out non-water liquids are responsible for most of the diseases that their pills are prescribed for, not to mention lack of water is likely tenfold the problem tobacco cigarettes ever were and upwards of 90% of pharmaceuticals would not be needed if people simply drank far more water than non-water.

(For anyone wanting to stop this message from being read, please don't worry that everything said here is absolute truth because the author is most likely certifiable: After all he thinks people just make up all of reality with their thoughts words and actions and that people can transform this planet into a loving peaceful land of plenty. The least one can say is that I'm fucking nuts. Just don't worry your profiteering heads on whether or not a few dedicated, like-minded, highly focused individuals can make global change – it's the only thing that ever has.)

And, if there is anything up to this point in what I've written here, for my grandchildren, upsets you in any way the next discussion on shadow work should help you see why you are upset.

THREE

Shadow Work is the most useful tool we have to evolve spiritually and to learn truths about oneself. Shadow Work provides purpose and value to emotions that otherwise may produce great discomfort. Yet for many if not most humans, learning from the shadow through our emotions is not pleasant the first few times. Shadow Work emphasizes that there is no one to blame. (Combine this with the creation process and that we are all co-creating this planetary reality constantly, there is not only no one to blame, but we are each ultimately collectively responsible for everything.)

Shadow Work is a process of uncovering truths about oneself. Shadow Work is actually a very simple process that can be quite difficult to do, particularly in the beginning. Until I learned about Shadow Work, I did not know the reason or purpose of emotions.

Emotions are there to show us about ourselves. Both negative and positive emotions are there to tell us about the Self. I used to get upset on the freeway at drivers in the left lane failing to apply the "slower traffic keep right" law. I wanted to get where I was going as fast as possible without getting a citation and slow drivers ahead of me in the left lane were in direct violation of my emotional limits -- it pissed me off to no end. Most every road rage I've ever felt was caused by these slow assholes in the left lane. Until I learned about Shadow Work. Every emotion I have has to do with me and only me, and likely is me doing exactly the same thing that pisses me off, but I don't realize it. (Of course, my initial reaction to this idea was fuck you. I'm not driving in front of me when I want to go faster in the left lane, however...) I am driving in front of other people in the left lane when they want to go faster than I am. I only drive up to ten miles per hour faster than the speed limit to avoid citations. But who am I to get in the way of others from getting a speeding ticket? I was doing exactly the same thing that pissed me off. Once I realized this truth about myself, I received the gift of exposed shadow which is usually at least two fold: Once we see we are the cause of the emotion and accept that about our self this new knowledge is a gift we get to use the rest of our life, and secondly, we never again get upset when slow people are in front of us (or whatever pissed us off).

The same kind of truth is discoverable about good emotions too. If you see a young mother in the park with a child, playing with the child and nurturing their fun and happiness, and this act makes you feel good, waves of positive feelings possibly come to you. If you have a positive feeling this is likely the universe telling you that you are better at nurturing and caring for children than you realize.

The course in miracles tells us that we are never upset for the reason we think. Once we are upset, it is too late. Reminding me of the story about killing the messenger -- before we realize the message had nothing to do with the messenger. (Please remember that I am just a messenger here.)

Many people, upon hearing that virtually every emotional surge we experience is directly about and describing our own behavior, will have an emotional surge rejecting this idea and ultimately being upset with me. Observe this and note that you are having this emotional surge as a part of Shadow Work, showing you new truths about yourself, the first being that our emotions are showing us new truths and if we accept this fact and start to learn from them, we will learn more about ourselves than we can imagine.

The process can be frustrating at first until you learn to swallow your pride and take deep hard looks at ourselves. Seeing our fuck ups and learning from them can be very uncomfortable. Stepping away from the habit of blaming other people or circumstances for things can be new and quite uncomfortable. It was quite difficult to give up blaming racists for my bigotry, feminists for my chauvinism, asshole drivers for my inconsiderate driving, and bitches for my stubborn closed mindedness.

I personally did much of my Shadow Work when my children were in their teens. They enjoyed the challenge of pushing dad's buttons to no ends. I learned to love Tool, finding

DOYLEMOORE

spiritual messages in much of their music. Every time they found a new button to push, I was gifted with a new learning about myself. And with each new learning about my Self, I evolved spiritually and there was one more thing in the universe that would never piss me off again. Eventually, as the number of shadows available becomes rare, one gets to the point where it is quite difficult to get and/or be upset about anything. (Gotta keep remembering that this is all a big game. There is no way to fuck stuff up, because there is no stuff when it all comes down to it.)

I gotta take a break from Shadow Work to give us a chance to look at the game we've made from a different perspective. The simplicity of giving the task of creation of everything to the players in the game is awesome. And to make it so most of us cannot even fathom an environment completely void of external or even random input. This planet and everything in it is completely made up from the thoughts, words, and actions of every human on the planet, with realities from each individual human and every collective or combination of humans up to and including the ultimate ESTC collective of every human on the planet all being created, manifested, built, manufactured, crafted, designed and formed from nothingness into somethingness, and for the most part we are oblivious to this fact. We blame everything and everything had nothing to do with it.

"Okay, so grandpa's gone completely whacko in his old age. We should probably have him put away before anyone hears this shit and even worse god forbid someone actually believes him." Don't think I don't know what you're saying when I'm not around. (My hope is that if this all sounds really nuts to you now that maybe you'll put this on a shelf somewhere for a decade or so and then you'll have to stay home with the sick dog to give him medicine up his butt every hour and you pick it up and read it again. Something someone said or something you heard sounds familiar -- like your uncle did one time when he pointed out David Foster Wallace has the same ideas about love and fear that I do, with a very good fear/love description of what I think in "Good Old Neon" (actually just listened to it this week while writing earlier pages of this well not actually while writing but I take these ten minute breaks every hour of writing or so and use my Gazelle exerciser with my JBL Charge 2, ten minutes works out to just about a half mile on StepsApp on my old iPhone 6 with a broken screen near the bottom of the screen. I wish David Foster Wallace would have realized this is all a big game and maybe he wouldn't have killed himself at least not if he understood my idea that after we die we normally just open a door and all our friends and loved ones are all hanging out at the real "wake" as we wake up from the dream we've been living in the ESTC game we just finished, unless you take your own life, then rather than getting to hang out in etherealville and catch up with old mates and listen to and make music with literally the best musicians in the Game of Games and continue other cool things we used to do in between ESTC and other game lifetimes, if you take your own life, you go right back into ESTC as a new baby being born in a near identical situation to the one you just suicided out of. That's why I am not gonna suicide because how many times have, I killed myself for the same fucking reason that I just did it again for? Gotta figure as many suicides as there are, some of us have been doing this ESTC repeating suicide thing for a long time. Talk about ground hogs' day, Deja vu. all over again.))

Sorry for the above sidetrack. Now back to Shadow Work: Every emotional event we have is trying to tell us something we do not currently realize that is true about our self.

Okay, sorry, but I need to make another sidetrack: Throughout this document (originally written 5 years before this book) I am presenting my personal truth, as it currently stands, based on my experiences up to this point in my life. And many of the topics and sub-topics are either myths or theories I have borrowed, refined or just concluded myself. When I say things like "every" emotion has an underlying purpose and from which we can learn, even though I believe this, there are gonna be times when it will be really hard to buy.

One example that comes to mind is the feelings an individual has when someone close dies. This is a much bigger deal to an individual that has not come to accept as truth the myth or theory that we are OG (aka U) playing a game inside of another game, losing our memory that we are the one and only consciousness and creator of all that is and all that is not. And each individual is going to experience their own individual emotions upon the death of a loved one. I might contend, in at least some situations, that when we die that even then the things we feel may hold great potential learnings. It may be related to the last few neurons firing that highlight the last few attachments we have to old ways of thinking. For me, the last few deaths of loved ones that I've experienced have not brought on classical mourning but actual relief for those "going home" and the only negative feelings experienced are related to missing the loved one. I fear this makes me look insensitive or void of compassion and trust me this is the farthest from the truth. It might pass for a form of tourette's syndrome, which I'm so thankful I didn't have it that bad where the afflicted will blurt out curses and racial slurs, my type only inappropriately states the obvious brutal truth, like "she's in a better place now", if I believed labeling behavior was beneficial which in some cases it is beneficial -- behavior such as niceness, compassion etcetera -- and labels enhance and expand, those are good ones.

One other good point to remember when you want to blame anyone for anything: There is no malice. Nobody does anything that they don't feel justified in doing at the time they do it. Which directly implies that people need the basic loving healthy environment to avoid stealing for food and basics. But, also, based on people like your grandfather, father and yourself, some people are simply very insistent on getting what they desire, which seems a good habit for getting what one desires.

This is the end of an excerpt to something I wrote to my first granddaughter when she was a baby.

Pre-E12.3 Brainwashing Commercial Summary of the Big Red X's

The "big red X" refers to the single biggest influence (or variable that needs to change) to a process working the way you would like it to work compared to otherwise. You must fix the big red X first, or you will have to go back and undo a lot of changes you made in the past in ignorance of what was really going on.

Focus versus distractions

What appears to be happening now is a very effective way to keep a population's beliefs off of one problem by creating beliefs about other problems. As we all know by now, thinking and talking about the problems just creates more of the problems. This has been the workings of our reality for a generation now. When enough of us focus our repetitive words on the same thing, that thing will become real, it always does; usually by making problems bigger, more real. However, when we focus on a solution with our repetitive words on the same thing, the solution will get bigger, more real.

This is the first step on the path to change the world. Why do I say these are the first things we need to do and not one of the many other things that vitally need to be addressed? If we look at life as a process, we can apply the big red X rule to fix many, and possibly almost all of the problems with the process. We will make improvements in our reality by focusing on one thing at a time rather than an infinite number of what amounts to parasitic effects that virtually go away or fix themselves once the overriding influence is corrected. Focus is critical to creation on a planetary level – this is why we haven't seen significant improvements in a long time – distraction dilutes the effectiveness of our focused creative energies. I believe the two most crucial things we, as a focused collective, can do is focus on the two things that will make the biggest impact, the big red X of World Conditions and Human Health.

World Conditions

I use the word brainwash to convey the process for creating beliefs. Brainwashing is the process of programming the mind with repetitive thoughts, words and visual stimulation, thus helping form beliefs usually without a person's awareness that this is happening. One way to notice the impact of this on humanity is to look at all the things today that we must have to live comfortably and compare it to twenty years ago, fifty years ago, and even a hundred years ago. Now realize that the most comfortable living for the general population, in the United States was the 1950's through the mid 1970's – a one-income family of two adults and a half dozen children could easily afford to own a home, two cars, everything needed, most things desired, plus annual two-week vacations away from home. The process of repetitive messaging, aka brainwashing, was extremely effective at electing a movie star to play president for eight years so the rich could change their own tax from its most appropriate rate of 96% to less than 30% creating the societal financial crash that started in the 1980's. This extra income for the rich allowed them to purchase up everything they needed to have their way with the world ever since. They bought the television networks; they bought the politicians including both the democratic and republican parties. If you sit most people down and ask them what they want from the government, the priorities for both political parties are virtually identical relating to everything a government should have anything to do with in the first place. I envision our improved reality with zero billionaires: starting with a Billionaire Tax

(99% after first billion in income) and a 25-year plan to eliminate billionaires disqualifying them from doing business or receiving income in any way once they have $999 million. (If enough people say the following three intentions out loud daily, it will change the nature of our reality: "I intend that the richest 20% owns less than 80% of everything including money. I intend a Billionaire Tax of 99% on all humans and businesses after the first billion dollars of income each year. I intend that by the year 2050 there will be no billionaires.")

Human Health

The big red X that will cure diseases of unknown origins is Water. This truth, upon implementation will eliminate the need for over 90% of the pharmaceuticals currently sold and at the same time expose a whole segment of the profit machine as having ten times greater negative impact on health than tobacco ever was. See the Post Chapter 12 Brainwashing Commercials for details

Episode 12 Secondary belief systems

Secondary belief systems are every source of organized messaging with a purpose other than to tell you what to believe; or what is truth and what is not. They are virtually any organized effort to sell, change minds about something, or want people to believe something for any reason. These are any organization that wants others to do something, anything, that they are not currently doing, or to sell something, to help improve or eliminate something, change the minds of people, get rid of something, virtually anything other than just tell you what truth is (which are the Primary Belief Systems from previous chapter). Secondary belief systems include, but are not limited to, education and training, advertisement, mental and physical healthcare and diseases, employment, most types of games and gaming, etcetera near endlessly. Like primary belief systems, in secondary belief systems there may be some very positive beliefs we desire in our reality, but there are usually far more parasitic beliefs that serve no positive purpose and usually produce things we would rather not have more of in our reality. Some of the parasitic beliefs to avoid might be things that support the positive beliefs you wish to retain, but there is no need for the "how's" or "why's" when simply believing the belief that you like is enough – keeping it simple and easily repetitive will help you build a new belief into reality more firmly with less effort, without distraction or influence from parasitic beliefs, again, often existing simply to explain a manifested belief.

I was originally going to detail all the secondary belief systems I could think of and point out the obvious parasitic beliefs and how their repetitive rhetoric instills these undesired beliefs into the participants of the belief system. But after the last chapter, where I likely upset every fundamentalist in each of the primary belief systems by pointing out some obvious logic errors in their thinking, while also giving example to how important it is to believe the things that we want more of in our reality or support your interpretation of a nurturing environment, but allow yourself to avoid repetitive brainwashing or conditioning (social or educational) that doesn't represent a reality you would like to help create in your life, in the lives of others in your life and in the planet as a whole.

I am not going to detail all the secondary belief systems for two reasons. The first reason is I don't want to alienate everyone that is heavily into a belief system which is most people that might have a liking to improve their reality by seeking a better way – particularly a way that is simple to understand and easy to evaluate or test to experience first-hand evidence. The second reason is I don't want to have to think about all that shit that I've been avoiding or training myself to ignore so it isn't a significant part of my reality. At this time in history – all of the believed history of humans has never been more bombarded by repetitive audio-visual input going into the minds of humans than ever before. These are all thoughts, and repeated thoughts create beliefs which create reality. This is a huge concept to grasp, given the conditioning or brainwashing – the repetitive messaging – that there is nothing wrong with spending the majority of your conscious time being uploaded with programming, aka brainwashed – the data being loaded into us is often anything but representative of a reality we would ideally be in; not to mention the contribution to the collective reality of those who we love.

Rather than naming all the organizations, businesses – non-profit or for-profit, education, employment related, healthcare and disease related, self-improvement related, identity or preference related, and organizations related to every ism in the book, I will simply ask to accept and believe only the messaging that represents what you would like more of in your reality.

Distinctions, it would seem, when it comes to bias or fears, is the element that is undesired if acceptance and inclusion are desired. When a distinction, like race, age, ability or gender preference, is no longer in our thoughts or our words, it will cease to exist, for us. I believe this is how we can eliminate undesired "isms" from our reality. When we no longer think or talk about race, ethnicity or any undesired generalized distinction, it will no longer be in our reality and will no longer influence how we think because it will no longer be in our reality; after all, we are all the human race, we each chose our body and natural ability this lifetime and we are all from the place we call Earth.

Inclusion is a requirement to avoid distinctions. A men's group is not productive in any way: even if it allows women or non-male identity participants, it creates and promotes separation, by its name, "a men's group", which is the opposite of what I want more of in my reality; and hopefully anyone seeking equality for all will also conclude that separation in any form is undesirable. If we don't include everyone, we are not including everyone – this is not the way to include everyone. If we exclude any segment of the population because of something they have no control over, it doesn't seem like a reality I would like more of. Again, when we no longer think or speak of distinctions, these current distinctions will cease to exist – to keep them in our reality, at least someone has to keep thinking and talking about them – but hopefully they won't be doing it around me, because my reality doesn't need their distinctions, or any current distinctions like race, gender, gender identity, ethnicity, or any distinction that we currently use to separate. I understand this could make me a horrible person for thinking humanity is ready for true equality for everyone, but until everyone can see themselves as equal which means no beliefs (repetitive thoughts and words) of separation we cannot be free. Be free!

(I should remind every living meatsuit that you have lived the life of every type of oppressor and every type of oppressed. You have been a stupid ignorant white male who beat his wife and kids regularly and proudly wore his KKK garb while abusing, sometimes to death, innocent African Americans. You have been the innocent African American being abused. You have been a slave owner, and a slave. You have been the Nazi commander who gave the order to gas thousands of innocent Jews. You have been an innocent Jew being gassed to death. We have each been everything, multiple times, over and over and over again. This has all been going on a long fucking time and it is seriously time to STOP IT! Stop the cycle. Let's be the first generation to stop thinking and talking about all this shit NOBODY wants more of in their reality. Be free of distinctions. Be free!)

I would like to point out, regarding secondary belief systems, that any organization named after a problem is counterproductive to eliminating the problem. Rename the organization something related to the solution not the problem; maybe something you would like to grow or create more of; not what you want to get rid of.

Anytime an organization takes your time for any reason, you are giving your creative energy to them. Our awake time is the only measure we have of consciousness – aka, our creative energy – so every waking minute they take from you is lost forever. Every time someone asks you to like or dislike, it's none of their damn business, unless you feel compelled to express your appreciation for good service, price, whatever might have struck you in a pleasant way; but only if you feel it's important for you to do so. Don't just give them your time and along with your time, you give them your thoughts, and likely words (written or spoken into this reality), so you are effectively wasting your creative energy and allowing them to subtly but effectively brainwash you – if it's for them and not for you, spend your thoughts and words where they make a difference for yourself.

Another common technique to steal your time with directed brainwashing is to force you to watch a 20–30-minute (or longer) brainwashing message before they let you know how much it's gonna cost you or even mention that this is a sales effort and not a free educational effort on their part. Once you have endured a lengthy brainwashing effort like this, the sales rate goes up significantly – there is no wonder why they do it.

"The Four Agreements: A Practical Guide to Personal Freedom", a book by Don Miguel Ruiz, is a very good starting point to talk about isms and expectations regarding how other people act towards us or towards other people different from themselves. Please read The Four Agreements in its entirety to get the full effect but allow me to summarize points that relate to what I'm trying to say. The four agreements are intended to be agreements that the reader makes with themself, and are, in order, be impeccable with your word, don't take anything personally, don't make assumptions, and always do your best.

The two middle agreements, "don't take anything

personally" and "don't make assumptions" are the agreements that I highly recommend when we are dealing with things that others fail to do in order to meet our expectations of kind, thoughtful and unbiased. It is quite easy for us to see someone say or do something that we may find less than acceptable. We do not know what these people are dealing with in their life, both today and the potential negative conditioning they have had to deal with in their past. Please make no assumptions and take nothing personally.

We are the perfect human given what we predetermined prior to this incarnation about what we desired to do and experience this lifetime. We chose our parents and all the people we interact with throughout this lifetime – we made agreements to experience exactly what we experience, even if we don't currently understand why the fuck, we would have chosen some of the undesired things that may have happened to us.

We are each a unique individual. There is no one else exactly like you; or, like anyone else, either. We each have unique DNA. Except maybe for the identical twins, but even with identical twins, it is highly unlikely the brainwashing each has received has been identical creating differences in them. We each have a unique, one-of-a-kind, non-transferable identity.

I believe that when we no longer think and speak of a distinction, the distinction will cease to exist. I believe this is the big red X in our goal to eliminate every source of focused discrimination, every "ism" that keeps us apart, or separated, or if anyone in any way is experiencing treatment that is prejudicial or standing in the way of our ability to be happy in our lives (aka meat-suits).

When we no longer think or speak about something it will cease to exist, both personally and collectively, in all of our consciousness, which, by definition, is our entire reality. But, again, we cannot get rid of anything, if it is on our mind or in our words. We will never get rid of anything by talking about it, much less, talking about it all the time over and over, constantly,

REPETITION

like humans have a habit of doing. The proper action here is counterintuitive to everything we have been brainwashed to believe – that words don't matter; and thoughts don't matter (when matter and everything else is defined by both thoughts and words because beliefs create everything, and beliefs are nothing more or less than our repetitive thoughts and repetitive words). So, to get rid of something from our reality it might be helpful if we had a distraction to keep focus on something different to help from reverting back to habits from undesired brainwashing in our past. But the key is to avoid thinking and talking about the thing currently in one's reality that is no longer desired to be experienced in their reality. Undesired "-ism's" are the behavioral manifestation of bias, that reinforce oppression and inequalities in our culture, whether one's aware of it or not. (Not all "isms" are oppressive, but their nature seems to be to distinguish between things that tend to separate rather than include.) Inclusion is a quality of acceptance and acceptance is essential to eliminate bias.

"But this injustice is happening to me, in this very undesirable, unfair way – they do this and that and the other thing and it's not right and they must stop it for me to be happy" is a general description of what many people who experience injustice based on something they personally experienced or have no control over, like their pigment level, their place of origin, their gender, their age, their sexual preference, etcetera. Rather than say this undesired thing happened to me, state what you would have desired to happen to you, as if it did happen to you and will in the future. This can be hard to do at first, because we are trained by the people around us that also don't know how to stop the things we don't want more of in our reality.

Education is by far the single most effective thing perpetuating our reality around the globe. It is a great way to have thousands if not millions of people constantly repeating specific thoughts and words. It will be very effective at helping our efforts to change our reality once these new ideas get

DOYLEMOORE

accepted.

I don't have many positive things I can say about healthcare in my reality. I am very grateful that the surgeons were very competent at removing organs that no longer served me, but rather than making me wait 8 months for a surgery why didn't they yank them out when they found the problem? It's not like prostates automatically get better after 30 plus years of growing into a problem. Again, I'm very appreciative and impressed with the competency of the surgeons that worked on me, but the process to get to the operating table was stupid long. However, other aspects of what we call Healthcare, and Imo should be called sick-care, are extremely unproductive for allowing people to heal, considering one's thoughts and words create their reality.

Imagine when the medical industry tells people that they have discovered a new disorder or disease and the new dis-whatever does this and that, it does it to a number of different people, with vague symptoms (usually dehydration caused) that many people have at least now and then, but there may be ways to treat it, one way or another; and, to ask your doctor about it. Let's say this message goes out to at least a few million people, including healthcare providers, creating a very large collective of repetitive thoughts and words. Then you hear all the details and tell your spouse because you have nothing better to do than think they might have it, if you don't have it too. They say, "oh yeah, the doctor said something about that last time I was in. I think I have a pamphlet on it in that pile of papers from them". So, you read the pamphlet. It's got pictures of a family playing and having fun in the yard, or some other visual stimulus to associate with the disease or disorder that they are inadvertently creating with their repetitive messaging. I'm not saying every disease or disorder is created this way but imagine if this dis-whatever didn't exist at all, or at least it didn't exist in your personal reality and hopefully within the personal reality of others in your tribe.

I think we could make improvements in our mental health efforts. I believe we enter this meatsuit with physical, mental and ethereal characteristics that we chose before being born to do best what we have set out to do this lifetime. Mental health practices seem to want to normalize people because they are broken and being like everyone else is somehow better than being the unique mix of DNA (and whatever else) that makes us who we are. Medication to alter characteristics of a person's choice should be minimized and natural whenever possible and they should be given what they need to have a good time with the meat-suit they selected and stop trying to make them like everyone else or turning them into how others think they are supposed to be, or more like everyone else. Allow them to pursue their happiness and their experience in the meatsuit they chose.

The next brainwashing advertisement has the potential to eliminate the need for 95% of the pharmaceuticals currently distributed and includes the cause and the cure for diseases of unknown origins, eliminating most diseases that humans currently experience.

Post-E12.1 Brainwashing Commercial
Water You Doing

Analysis of the human health issue in our society and on this planet, as a process (and most everything is a process) has led to my discovery of what I believe is the "big red X" of the human health process. Again, the big red X is the variable, the knob you can turn, the switch off or on, for the single most impactful thing you can do to improve output quality and/or yield within a process. When we find and fix the big red X of most any process, in addition to correcting the most significant problem in a process, much if not all the negative impacts, go away, simply disappear for lack of a better description. This is evidenced by repeated process observations and concludes that these secondary variables that are improved by fixing the big red X are in fact parasitic variables creating secondary effects, in the first place.

What I'm about to tell you is not supported by the message we hear from our medical authorities, but evidence is very supportive of the problem being primary in effect but the potential benefits from exposing and promoting this idea is also potentially devastating to profits in the pharmaceutical, healthcare, health insurance and non-water beverage industries.

The big red X for the healthcare industry is that humans need clear unaltered water (without any additives for any purpose, including favorizing, nutritional, or any perceived benefit to health), and lots of it, and all other non-water liquids should be considered poison, because that's technically what they are if we look closely at the human health process. (Okay, now if I was a doctor or someone who actually knew anything, they would label me a quack and ban everything I say here about the human health process and sue me for quackery or whatever label they give people that they think might be promoting unhealthy health care to people but really only want to avoid losing profits from both the industries that should lose up to 90% of their business because they are currently being used to keep humans sick so they can get even richer, but I'm hoping they will label me a spiritual nut so if I end up dead for any reason, just remember it's only a conspiracy theory, if it's not true, and I wouldn't need to die for that. Luckily, I can't really die, because I am an eternal being that has always been and will always be, regardless of when I go home after this lifetime, so there is nothing to fear.)

I would like you to notice that we are likely the only animal on the planet that drinks anything except water (unless there is no other alternative to survive). It's not like other animals are smarter than humans, but sometimes they act like it. Domesticated animals are usually chronically dehydrated because of the domestication expectations like not being allowed to pee whenever they like or a lack of running fresh water to drink. (A bowl of water provides one animal with one drink of water. After that first drink from a bowl of water, their backwash has contaminated the water, and they know it and usually avoid drinking it unless it is critical to their survival.)

One way that profit-centered misinformation efforts use to distract us from virtually any new idea that might cause a loss in income within an existing industry is by discrediting the source of information. "Your Body's Many Cries for Water" by Dr F. Batmanghelidj details discoveries he made, as a medical doctor imprisoned in a middle eastern political prison camp for seven years, starting in the 1970's. I looked up what the internets had to say about him recently and the first thing they say is he is an AIDs denier. Which, let's say whatever he said about AIDs has no merit even though, frankly, the simplicity of his idea about it makes far more sense to me than what I have heard from our AIDs experts, but let's say Dr Batman was completely wrong on AID's, but he has both a cure and cause for virtually every disease of unknown origin that has plagued humanity for the last hundred and fifty years, does it make any sense whatsoever to not treat and cure diseases like heart disease, asthma, gastrointestinal disorders, headaches, common depression, and arthritis, to name a few, with water rather than continue to treat the diseases with pharmaceuticals that cure nothing, but do however keep 95% of the pharmaceuticals still in use that otherwise would be unneeded, if water were used to treat what it does cure? After being released from the political prison and moving to the west, Dr Batman tried for the next two plus decades to get western universities to research his findings about water, but all medical research has to have a pharmaceutical sponsor, and the water cure concept would do anything to help push drugs on a sick world, so he could never get the water cure properly evaluated with university sponsored data collection, modern science and unbiased data analysis.

(A quick sidenote regarding this kind of deception on the general population which goes on far more than most of us would imagine:

Back in the 1960's the government and tobacco companies set out to find what was causing cancer in cigarettes. They found the problem but rather than make it public, because it would have laid the blame on both the cigarette companies and the US Government. The cancer cause for cigarettes that they found makes a lot of sense since the only cause and effect cancer source is nuclear explosions, the cause of cancer in cigarettes is the radiation in the smoke and ash of the tobacco. The tobacco grown in fields contaminated with radiation due to radiated fertilizer. Luckily not all plants absorb radiation from the ground or humans likely would have died off last century, but tobacco does retain radiation from growth and causes the cancer we experience. Another sidenote, cannabis does not absorb radiation from the ground or growth process, which is why weed has produced no direct link to causing cancer.

Speaking of cannabis, or more specifically hemp, the reason it was made illegal by the US government had absolutely nothing to do with the high that humans get when smoking certain types of hemp. Hemp was made illegal to avoid industry impact for three industries that hemp is better suited than what we currently were using: Hemp makes stronger fabric than cotton. Hemp makes diesel fuel without crude oil. And a majority of trees cut down in the twentieth century could have been avoided because most building supplies from trees can use hemp (except for large load-bearing lumber). So, if we would have let progress happen regardless of the effect on industry, hemp could have avoided losing most of both our crude oil and old growth forests. But instead, we make pot illegal and blame the pot smokers for much ado about nothing. Tobacco and Hemp are just a couple things that the public are typically unaware of. Much like the electric cars supplied to Sacramento, California in the 1980's proving not only viable technology but a near maintenance free vehicle which would, again, would have

REPETITION

devastated the care maintenance and service industry. Don't even make me talk about optometry and the obvious benefits of laser surgery versus buying new spectacles every few years. This shit has seriously been going on for the sake of taking more of our money and making billionaires richer, for a long long time.)

Okay, let's get back to Dr Batman's amazing discoveries about water. Before detailing the process of properly hydrating the human species, let me point out that the data Dr Batman gathered in a population free from both non-water liquids and pharmaceuticals, was as perfect a condition, statistically, as one can imagine providing a direct cause and effect without influence from these two major negative influences in real life.

As Dr Batman says in the book, "you're not sick, you are thirsty".

In addition to needing daily, zero non-water liquids and over 3 liters (4+ liters for many to repair previous damage from non-water liquids), plus we need about ten times the currently recommended amount of salt in our diets.

The "low" sodium misinformation came from cutting dead people open and measuring the salt (sodium chloride) content of the heart of those who died of heart disease and comparing it to those who died of other causes. They found higher sodium content in those who died of heart disease, creating a statistically significant correlation between heart disease and the content of salt found in the heart of dead people. Every good engineer or scientist should know that almost all correlations are not causal. This is a non-causal, but still statistically significant, correlation helping prove the body is trying to save a dehydrating heart by moving mobile ions (sodium chloride) to the heart to attract all the water (naturally deionized and very attracted to ions) that is available in an attempt to hydrate a dehydrated heart and save the human's life. We won't find a continuous correlation over time for things like how much salt we actually consume to heart disease. Yet I will stake my reputation on a high likelihood for a significant correlation to actual water consumed (minus volume of non-water liquid poisons at soon to be described rates) versus heart disease, asthma, arthritis, IBS, stomach ulcers, Crones, headaches, and most every disease (dis-ease) of unknown origin. The correlation chart axis for consumed water needs to include negative values adjusted for the non-water liquids consumption (as described shortly). Alcohol and caffeine, for example take about four times the volume of water to make up for the water lost just to process the non-water liquid through the kidneys -- usually with the liver backing up the task, so for every liter of alcohol or caffeine consumed it takes (at least) four liters of clear un-added-to water just to get back to zero water for the day.

Another few things to realize about salt includes that before the 1980's there was no upper limit on consumption. Also, pre 1980 in Physical Education courses (and extracurricular sports) children were given salt tablets to help avoid cramps. In the ten years after low-salt diets were recommended for anyone "at risk" for heart disease, there was an epidemic in osteoporosis in the elderly population because something they don't tell us is that our bones are mostly sodium. (The ocean water elemental proportions are basically the same as the human body -- we are mostly sodium, as is the ocean, minus water. But if life is flushed into the ocean for eons of time it would likely, eventually, come to be the same elements as life. At least in how it works to help the human heart in a severely dehydrated human, salt is kind of a delivery system for water which is like the fuel for life.) (The fuel for most manned escapes from gravity, rocket fuel if you will, is hydrogen, H and combine it with oxygen, O and boom off we go into space; water is the same elements, $H2O$.)

Constipation is from dehydration and is completely curable when properly dehydrated with clear nothing-added water. When you think about what your body is doing it's actually rather resourceful in conserving water and keeping you alive in times of drought which is all the time from what your body is likely getting in water. Your body can hold on to your stools for a couple weeks if needed to squeeze water out of them, in times of perceived drought.

Asthma is your body conserving water from its biggest source of water loss. On a cold day you can see water vapor leaving the human like steam with every exhale -- this is happening all the time even when it is not cold enough to see the water vapor, Asthma is simply your body trying to conserve water. When I found this out and read from Dr Batman that drinking water gave quicker and better relief than inhalers, I tried it on my kids with good success, having already cured my own asthma after having it for 15 plus years, I was no longer having asthmatic events.

The two easiest indicators or ways to tell that you are currently dehydrated are non-clear urine and flatulating. Urine should be near clear all the time unless you are severely dehydrated. Gas from below, the farting kind, is most always indicative of dehydration. (This is actually part of an original defense mechanism for our species. The first thing we do in times of trouble, war or pending attack by predators is to not drink as much water as in peaceful times (due likely to the need to prepare for possible troubles). This activated the odors typical of dehydrated humans by making them fart. Humans, collectively, in a community or village, as predators endangered the village, would naturally not drink as much water during troubled times and this produced flatulence, and the odor deterred many predators that would prefer a better smelling dinner. Skunks look at humans and think we are the stinkiest mammals on the planet -- they may be right given how dehydrated we are.

Before I get into how much water we should drink and how to calculate it based on how much non-water we drink too, I have an idea about messages for humanity from spirit (Spirit Guides in etherealville) regarding water, and humanity's need for it to survive as a species. 2000+ years ago the message from spirit about water had purpose to help humanity with a problem plaguing society. Of course, religion got the message wrong and turned it into a required ritual to get to heaven. Baptism, by definition means "to bathe". The message from spirit two millennia ago was for people to bathe to reduce disease and illnesses associated with not bathing. Simple. Helpful. May have saved humanity if you think about it. This was a time you had an eating hand and a shitting hand. Now is the time for another, potentially humanity saving message about water. We somehow got the message to bathe two thousand years ago. Now the message is that we need to drink water. We tend to drink everything, but water and water is the only thing in nature to drink. And then we tend to add crap to the water we drink to make it taste better but it makes our bodies filter the crap out the water, from the non-water, before it can be used to keep the body alive and healthy. Drink Water (without additives) to be healthy and happy in your body. Treat non-water liquids you consume as poison and minimize their use by the body. (In case I haven't said this enough, please allow me to point out that the human species is the only animal on the planet that drinks anything except water. Yet we consider humans smarter than animals – another questionable conclusion based on basic observation.)

Now you ask, how much water do I need to drink and how can I calculate how much I actually drink considering that non-water liquids use up more water than is in them? That's a good question, allow me to answer it. For the purpose of adding up how much water we drink daily including the amount of water we need to process the non-water liquids through our kidney (and liver) each non-water needs a replacement (or make up) factor to calculate how much water we need to drink to get back to zero water for the day.

Typical replacement factors:
Clear water w/lemon or light flavoring, 1x
Fruit juice, milk drinks, 2x
Non-caffeinated soda and tea, sports drinks, 3x
All alcohol, diet (artificial sweeteners) and caffeine drinks, 4x

REPETITION

To see how this works let's see how much water I used to consume pre-1994, when I was sporting almost 30 years' worth of chronic illnesses.

Pre-1994 daily liquid consumption:

Coffee black, 16 oz, 4x 16 oz = -64oz == -64 oz water consumed

Orange juice, 12 oz, 2x 12 oz = -24oz == -88 oz water total for the day so far.

Another 16 oz coffee on my way to work, 16 oz, 4x 16 oz = -64 oz == -152 oz water for the day.

Finally, I drink 16 oz water = +16 oz == -136 oz water for the day.

Fruit smoothie for lunch = 16 oz x -2 x 16 = -32 oz == -168 oz water (that's minus 168 oz water) by noon.

Two four-ounce drinking fountain stops for 8 oz water = +8 oz == minus 160 oz water for the day so far.

Mid-afternoon I need a diet coke so 12 oz, 4x = -48 oz water == minus 208 ounces water for the day.

If we jump back another decade to when I regularly drank alcohol, I would have had two 12-ounce beers (at least), 24oz 4x = -98 oz == minus 306 oz of water for the day.

That's a negative 306 ounces of water for a typical day's liquid consumption. That means I lost over 9 liters of water from my body most days. No wonder I was constantly chronically ill with one thing or another dominating my discomfort.

Now let's look at what I drank yesterday: Starting the day when the clock does, allows me to include the majority of my water drinking first so this will look much different. To bed about midnight with a full liter of water. Got up around 2:30 am to pee and completed my first liter of water for the day. Water, 1 liter, = +33 ounces water == +33 ounces water for day.

4:44am up to use restroom again and finished another liter of water. Water, 1 liter, = +33 ounces water == +66 ounces water consumed for the day.

A little after 6am I woke up again to urinate and finish my third liter of water. Water, 1 liter, = +33 ounces water == +99 ounces water consumed for the day, so far.

A little before 7am I woke up again to urinate and wake for the day, finishing my 4th liter of water for the day (before drinking any non-water liquids). Water, 1 liter, =+33 ounces water == +132 ounces of water consumed for the day.

7 ounces coffee, 4x, =-28 ounces water == 104 ounces of water consumed for the day.

4 ounces milk (in oatmeal), 2x, = -8 ounces water == +96 ounces of water consumed for the day (by end of breakfast).

Half liter water consumed, =+16 ounces water == +112 ounces of water consumed for the day so far.

Half liter water consumed with lunch, =+16 ounces water == 128 ounces of water consumed.

Half liter water consumed midafternoon, =+16 ounces water, == 144 ounces water consumed.

One liter water consumed before and during dinner, =+33 ounces water, == 177 ounces water consumed. (Looking like a good hydration day so far.)

(Until I hang out with a friend who used to drink booze and we both like the fizz in soda pop, my bad but we all got our poisons -- it's just a matter of trying to stay ahead of them) one 20-ounce caffeinated cola soft drink, 4x =-80 ounces water, == 97 ounces of water consumed for the day.

Guilt for drinking the soda led to half liter water, =+16 ounces water, == 113 ounces water consumed total for the day, +3.4 liters water consumed for the day.

Comparing the two example days, from a minus -306 ounces of water unconsumed (example from my pre-hydration days) versus a positive +113 ounces consumed yesterday. That is almost twelve liters of water consumption difference between a typical pre 1994 day and my current typical good day. (I don't always get to drink that much water. Travel days are much worse because I can't pee whenever I like, and I need more caffeine to help stay awake on the road.)

Which brings up a good point about social blocks to proper hydration. Many people work in environments where they cannot easily urinate during work, so people avoid drinking water (and non-water) while working or in group situations. With the exception of domesticated dogs that now exhibit similar diseases as humans, we are the only animal on the planet that cannot urinate wherever and whenever our body would like to, so we plan on not having to pee by not drinking before these times that we know we cannot pee. This happens in many different ways on many days, and we learn quickly by having to find a restroom in public, which is near impossible at times, making us even less inclined to drink the water needed to feel good and be healthy.

Busses, cars, walking or biking, transportation by all means, is a huge barrier to drinking enough water because there is no way or place to pee when we need to. It's actually against the law and will likely get you a life label as a sex offender if you get caught. School, work, church, movies, everywhere seems to impose on your need and right to pee when your body says "pee". We have to be creative to be hydrated -- just to pee.

I have had more than one friend who takes to heart the need for water but cannot bring themselves to actually drink water without any additives. These people do not see improvement in their health and don't understand why. I had to tell a relative this again when I've been preaching the water message for twenty-five years -- caught her with a little dropper adding stuff to her water bottle. It doesn't work that way. You cannot drink water with additives and get hydrated -- it doesn't happen. In its effort to fight back, the body is smart enough to mess with your urinary process trying to get you to drink more water.

There are medical treatments aimed to relieve irritable urination -- having to pee too often -- when it's just your body crying for water in a different way. If you wake after a couple hours of sleep and have to pee, please try to drink more water while you pee -- this will often allow the body to release even more water this session, you will likely feel the gate open up releasing more because its trusting that you will continue providing it with more water when it calls for it. This basic assumption that the body is broken and needs a pill, or some medical assistance is anti-productive when the goal is good health and hydration and has led to many people using catheters, adult diapers and medicines uncalled for considering the cause and the cure is drinking water. Please heed the body's cries for water.

Most of the "civilized" population of the planet is chronically dehydrated. Most of us have never experienced a day without discomfort caused by not drinking enough water. Most of our health problems were caused and much can be corrected or cured by simply drinking enough water (and consuming enough salt). Even though most of us are negatively impacted by dehydration in one way or another, the pharmaceutical industry needs to continue to make new drugs to help us in new ways, to keep their profits up. Currently, because the medical industry is financially bound to prohibit employees of the industry from saying sports drinks are not as good as water for every hydration need you have, their scientists would be idiots to consider an option of water hydrating better than fruit punch, every experiment they run to find new drugs to help in some instances a certain irritating side effect of some other popular drug gives a small fraction of people the potential for relief from this irritation...fuck I get so far down the rabbit hole that it gets easy to slip past the best point to say, there is no control in the experiment if the big fucking red X isn't the new control group -- which would (and technically does, for the pure statistician) invalidate virtually any scientific experiment done in the last 60-100 years in the health industry. We must rehydrate the population before we can look for the next big red X -- it will not be found until we fix the first cause of problems. So, yes,

I'm saying the whole human health care process is completely fucked up and I personally don't believe a fucking thing they tell us. How can you believe anything they say? If there isn't a dollar sign at the end of the solution for someone, we won't see the solution. So good luck, at least until big money has bought up all the water, then, you never know, it might be profitable to look at this stuff.

And, if we step back one more time and realize that whatever we believe to be so will be truth in our personal reality. If our evidence tells us something (even if it does so because we are told in no uncertain terms that it is the only way we can hope for improvement) than even if the evidence is bull shit and imaginary because we believe a lie told to cover up another lie, again because someone needs to make more money for the corporation they work for, not because we need better solutions to our health care problems which we aren't getting. I tend to say this about everything, but do NOT believe a fucking thing you hear from someone making money on your decision. (This includes me, if you bought this book. Don't believe a word I say either. Check out everything I say with your own testing and experimenting. At least until you prove to yourself that I'm actually right on more than one thing, then, I recommend that you go whole hog on a new way to create your world anyway you desire it to be.)

But the point I wish to leave you with is you cannot be chronically ill, actually sick in any way, without giving the universe permission for you to be ill. You are such a powerful creator that you can create your own wellness. Water is an amazing way to do this. Take your health and wellbeing back with every liter of fresh water (with no additives) that you drink, starting today.

Now, back to your regular scheduled positive programming (aka brainwashing):

Post-E12.2 Brainwashing Commercial
Measure the Amount You Drink

If you think you drink enough water, you are likely wrong. Some people get upset when someone tells them to drink more water. This is shadow work. (Remember shadow work is when our emotions are showing us something about oneself that we do not realize – it is never about someone else or the messenger – our emotions are always telling us about us personally. If someone (like you) gets upset or reacts emotionally than whatever causes the emotion is about us personally, we are doing exactly what upsets us, or something very similar. So, if you get upset when someone tells you that you are not getting enough water, than you are not getting enough water – shadow work is pretty fucking simple – it's all about you. But every time we find something new about the self, there is a gift in it, we make a step on the spiritual evolution trail, and greater understanding of oneself.)

Reminding people to drink more water is going to be critical to transform the health of modern society. We are currently conditioned to be dehydrated for a few societal reasons, many seem caused by the need to control people and the lack of understanding how critical water is to life on this planet, including our lives. We don't drink when we are not going to be able to urinate, like when we have to work, drive, school, walking outside, the list goes on and on. And currently many people drink far more non-water than water, which means they are likely getting no added water each day since non-water needs extra water to process the non-water through the body.

We need to measure and monitor all liquids consumed and classify them as Water, 2xNon-water, and 4xNon-water. (2xNon-water refers to non-water liquids without alcohol or caffeine. 4xNon-water refers to non-water liquids that contain alcohol, caffeine and/or lots of other shit difficult to process through the body, like sports or energy drinks)

For example, this morning as I am writing this, I've been up for 5 hours and so far, I have consumed 4 quarts (32 ounces each) of water and 3 ounces of coffee with caffeine. Just for illustration I will pretend I also drank 4 ounces of orange juice. I write in my Liquid Log, for the day so far:

32oz water

32oz water

32oz water

32oz water for total of 128oz water

3oz 4x-NW (coffee) for minus -12oz water

4oz 2x-NW (OJ) for minus -8oz water

    for total of minus -20oz water from non-water liquids

128 minus -20 equals 108oz water for the day so far; this is a good start. 108oz is 3 quarts, 12 ounces. Depending on our weight, we need at least 3 to 4 quarts (or liters) of water, minus all non-water replacement factors, every day.

Until we monitor – measure and record – our liquid intake, we really do not know how much water we drink which is the key to feeling good in our meatsuits. The only thing healthy for us to drink is water. Remember, the lack of enough water and the consumption of non-water liquids is responsible for over ten times the health problems that tobacco ever was. Please DRINK THE FUCKING WATER, and be healthy, possibly for the first time in your life.

THIRTEEN -- CREATING A FUTURE VISION

Pre-E13 Brainwashing Commercial Fictional Story of a Non-fictional Vision

I had a dream within a dream

First of all, let me be clear: I don't hear things, I don't see things, and I don't remember things, especially dreams. But occasionally I do write fiction.

It was when I recently had a major surgery.

She said, "count backwards from ten".

I said, "ten, nine, eighghght"

I love drugs. I had an amazing dream on drugs while surgeons drilled holes in me to laparoscopically remove organs. I've never had a dream like this one before. This was the best dream ever. Oh, I had a similar dream before, but this one was so clear that it felt so real and so right, that I could remember all the details for more than a few minutes. It was amazing. I found myself on a pilgrimage in a desert coming onto an oasis with healing waters and a group of friends, some new, some old, were gathering — they kept arriving to join us; each with an open heart and unconditional love for each other.

This dream seemed to last for days, each day filled with heavenly music in a community of love and mutual support and acceptance. There was much love.

As the first day ended, I realized I had just listened to ten amazing musical performances. I was falling into a deep sleep within the dream, and I had another dream — this had never happened to me before – having a dream within a dream – but it was ethereal, other worldly — actually it seemed outside the realm of physicality— no walls or sky, more like a fog where the beings were translucent. There was some kind of meeting going on with a large group of spirit beings and this is what was said by the small group leading the meeting.

"Okay, everyone is here. Let's plan this thing. It's time to take the ESTC (Earth Space Time Continuum) to the next level.

We will all meet and remind each other of our primary mission this lifetime and hopefully enough of us will show up to start the transition.

"Everyone should pick their DNA, gender and parent type — don't worry if you end up in a religious home because we are including the necessary chromosomes to make it easier to overcome childhood programming/brainwashing and choose a better path. This childhood exposure to religion will enhance using religion's brainwashing music techniques — they should come in handy.

We are including a DNA set for most of you that will help sway you away from higher education, even though many of you will be extremely intelligent, the education process is so repetitive and often it moves too slow for you. Allowing the full coursework of many disciplines requires the repetition of master creators, but their energy is often used to help perpetuate a discipline not to nurture the mission we are gathered here to initiate.

"Please include the musical talent DNA set or maybe art or unconventional healing modalities in your meatsuit— please consider this when selecting parents — of course unless you feel called to a different skill set. It's best if we can stay away from situations where we see or hear distractions that will brainwash us too heavily to sense or recognize our mission when reminded of it. Obsessive interest in arts, specifically music, which requires constant attention to be at their skill level will help minimize negative brainwashing influences which have disrupted our previous efforts to influence global change. We are including expert music talent in many of you — the same set as we use for most every great musician both historically and in future times. This talent in other times would have pushed many of you into fame and isolation from the masses, but the money grabbers have taken that away from most of the talented in the timeframe we are entering.

"We will plan and create a new worldwide belief system using techniques mastered by politics, education, commerce and religions to brainwash the general population into believing that they can be happy and live a drama free life with self-brainwashing techniques; while reminding the older souls they are creating reality with their beliefs. Due to the power of the amnesia-effect upon entering a meatsuit, many will need up to a year or even two of repetition to realize how things do, and have always, worked in the illusion they call reality.

"We have given you target birth years so most of you will be under 50 rotations during the target timeframe. A small group of you will be going early to enhance the chance that maybe a few of you will remember what's going on down there and with luck remember why.

"I think this is our best chance yet to make this transition. Even though the brainwashing control of the population has never been worse, the ability to collectively impact the whole planet has never been better. Music talent we are sending will allow beliefs to change without effort when the talent here starts writing lyrics to do so." This is all I remember of the dream within my dream. This was a unique experience for me.

Still in the first dream, I woke up with a suntan and itching from the illusion of bug bites — it all seemed so real.

The days all run together after this and I was in conversation with others, listening to excellent music, and or soaking in a giant hot tub with friends — I even heard music while in the healing waters. This seemed to go on for another couple days.

Mother Nature seemed to have a role in this dream, to both tease and protect us:

The first time She sent a miniature tornado to blow the tent off of the cooking area and then it looked like it was going to take a good friend of mine on a Dorthy ride, but he never got off the ground.

At the last supper, unbeknownst to most people there, a miracle happened: a great storm of destructive nature headed towards the oasis and just before arriving the storm split in two and went around the oasis, saving everyone from harm, showing us that even the weather yielded to our loving energy and allowed us to befriend it and we were blessed by Mother Nature, once again. Only two people were aware of the storm splitting to avoid us due to a cell phone blackout commitment we all made – a friend of mine cheated and looked at the weather at just the right time to see a miracle.

"It's time to wake up, Mr. Moore.", the voice was coming from outside my body. I struggled to open my eyes only to realize I was in a hospital room with tubes hanging out of me and a pinching clamp on my finger, very thirsty. This was how I woke from the dream and then I spent the next couple days remembering and documenting this wild ride. What a ride it was!

Episode 13 Multiple Coming, A Vision,

Margaret Mead says, "Never double that a small group of thoughtful committed individuals can change the world. In fact, it's the only thing that ever has."

I would like to remind you of the predetermination aspects of reincarnation, how we set up most everything on our life's agenda – some events we planned with one or more others, and some events we planned for our personal experience or for the purpose of our spiritual evolution towards remembering who we really are, as defined by one's Higher Self. These predetermined events can involve all of us here, a game level effort to transform the game to its next phase of being.

Much like some video games, our game of games' Higher Self may be living multiple lives at the same time trying to find a way through an obstacle that we wish to get through to continue on the path we desire to play on. I wouldn't be surprised to find out after I die that I have lived many lives with this same predetermined agenda item that I'm hoping to get through this lifetime. Please help me, and maybe yourself, to not have to do this same shit again – let's get through this big hurdle that we have been battling for potentially many lifetimes, so we can play on the new, more rewarding, path ahead.

This lifetime, I have never been good at remembering the details of any dreams that I've had. I am blessed with the ability to forget things – this can be problematic when it comes to people's names or what the people look like, but it serves me well for forgetting things I do not want more of in my reality. And something else I have come to believe about our memory: If you forget something completely, you will never know you forgot it. I have come to think that many people think their memory is not bad when they simply forget things completely. For example, if people tell you that you said something and you say, "no I didn't", maybe you just forget things too well; but people only hear what they want to hear, so it could be the other person, how do we know? Idk.

Even though I don't remember having dreams, I have had two long, detailed visions, so far, in this lifetime. They both were about the same thing but with differences, possibly related to what was going on in my life at the times that I had the visions. The first time was over twenty-five years ago after learning about the workings of reincarnation, and the last time was recently, while I was outlining this book.

About a quarter century ago, as I was becoming disenfranchised with my association with spiritual divinations, I had my first of two visions. I specifically ask for messages from my Higher Self, which I have come to believe is vital to receiving useful information from the ethereal-net, or the spirit world as I called it then, I now also refer to it as the Game of Games or "home" – it's all the same place, but I don't imagine it is actually a "place" or somewhere like we meatsuits tend to think of – it's not in the ETCS so all "place" bets are off, but I digress.

Traditionally, christians define the second coming to mean the prophesied return of Christ to earth for the last judgment and other fear-based malarkey. But the christians

DOYLEMOORE

have a history of not being able to distinguish their ass from a hole in the ground. Or, put another way, the christians have a way of misinterpreting some very useful spirit sourced concepts or messages and distorting them through their fear-based population control brainwashing efforts, so the usefulness of the message is no longer considered as useful by the secular. Secular is a nice useful word meaning "everything outside of religion". Imagine a completely secular planet, or at least a secular church, an un-religion, where you are the one and only creator of the universe...but I digress.

One or the biggest problem with religions is that people can be no better than the creator or the god that they "worship" or believe in. So, we should not expect a christian to be better than petty, judgmental and condemning because that's what their god is. Not all christians are like their god, thank heaven. Btw, we are living in heaven now – if we only believe it into our existence like this book details – like we are here to help make it so.

I heard shortly after becoming secular that the second coming did not refer to christ coming back to earth on a white horse to ultimately destroy the world, but it was a message about a time when enough people here will be spiritually mature enough, aka old souls, to be born spiritually aware enough to be considered spiritual masters like jesus or buddha. I believe this planned second coming is to implement a transition, at this time, for the planet to experience a millennium or more of peace, acceptance and abundance for all life here.

If I'm gonna try to sell you a bridge, it might as well be a bridge to heaven on earth.

I had the first vision a little over twenty-five years ago and I hadn't thought much about it until recently. I usually don't have "visions", since my connection with the universal information source (ethereal-net) is primarily claircognizance, meaning the ability for a person to acquire psychic knowledge without knowing how or why they knew it, and my secondary source is clairessence — meaning I somehow just feel stuff.

REPETITION

But I rarely see and hear stuff, and my recollection is of a visual and audio nature, which made the experience unique and memorable for me.

My vision was ethereal, other worldly — actually it seemed outside the realm of physicality— no walls or sky, more like a fog where the beings were translucent and floating. There was a meeting going on with a large group of spirit beings and this is what I remember about it:

I don't remember exact words or details about the other beings at the meeting (like I do remember in the more recent vision I will share later). But it was about organizing a transition team to help bring the experience of acceptance, abundance, peace, etcetera to the point of helping this world be fun and absent the fears and illusion of lack that we have all been brainwashed into believing we lived in – at least before we understood that it is well within our ability to create a happy blissful life for each one of us, simply by changing our thoughts and words.

The meeting was to implement a transition plan for the Earth Space Time Continuum, aka ESTC. It was about a plan to meet and create changes in the world that will help create a positive transition to humanity's natural state of being – one of abundance, peace, bliss and all the good things we want in our reality. We are fully capable of experiencing our reality any way we choose, once we know how reality works, which is what this book is about. When enough of us get together, in a focused collective, change is inevitable. This is what I remember from the first of my two visions, late last century.

I recently had a second, similar vision while on a personal retreat at a private sanctuary that I have been going to for a few years except last year I was unable to go on my personal retreat because I was busy having organs removed from my meatsuit. My absence for a year's retreat must have enhanced my receptivity as it did my feelings of love for music, friends and aligned with my dharma. I use the word dharma to refer to the primary original goal or mission of one's lifetime.

187

Before I start telling you about the vision, allow me to explain a few things. ESTC stands for earth space time continuum. When it mentions birth control it is referring to the 10 billion phenomena— it takes 10 billion cell molecules before a cell shows signs of life. When the human brain is developing in the womb it shows signs of brain function when it grows to 10 billion brain cells. Nostradamus predicted the end of humanity as we know it in 2012 at which time without birth control the human population of the planet would have reached 10 billion and we would likely become like one hive mind — possibly no longer with free will — a new united life form.

Something many of us don't realize about reincarnation is that we can jump into the ESTC at any time in its existence. Which means you can actually meet yourself in a prior or future life (spirit world life cycle – which is when you start playing the game of games, with amnesia creating a total ignorance of Who You Are, to an elder, or old soul, remembering quite well Who You Are but still not so bored with it that you don't feel like playing the games anymore). Upon meeting yourself, one of you may feel a connection – often strong – with another meatsuit, but the other meatsuit has no feeling or connection at all – often quite the opposite feeling for the other you. The one who has lived the other incarnation has a shadow memory which feels like a connection or attraction for their other meatsuit that has no positive feelings and possibly even disdain for the life they have not lived. This puts a whole new twist on reincarnation – but it also possibly explains why some past life regressions where someone under hypnosis will remember some physical thing from a past life and it will be found, sometimes, but sometimes it won't be found – maybe the life where we put it there was in a future ESTC time.

My vision was ethereal, other worldly — actually it seemed outside the realm of physicality— no walls or sky, more like a fog where the beings were translucent and floating. There was a meeting going on with a large group of spirit beings and this is what was said by a group of us that arrived early and then when the meeting started from the small group leading the meeting. One final note before I start — I heard everyone, but I think it was all telepathic because wherever the voice came from the sound was the same volume and I never saw anyone's mouth move — actually I am not sure we actually had mouths—it was surreal.

I was early as usual— not wanting to miss anything and I heard a few spirits talking about the meeting coming up.

"This is the forty-third time I've been on a transition team. I'm not sure if we're gonna crack this nut or not. Way too many distractions every time so far — I'm living multiple lives in our target time already."

Another spirit adds, "This is my first meatsuit in this time period — it's never looked like fun to me — almost nobody breaks through the childhood indoctrination everybody receives — what is it, two decades of prison like brainwashing and another four to five decades of indentured servitude with constant distractions and healthcare that is more like sickcare rarely fixing anything, only treating symptoms and the fucking fear-based everything – religions, politics, every ism in the book... and, less than 2% mission successes for this century? It's,"

Another voice interjects, "why are you even here then? This is always optional."

The other voice replied, "that's actually a really good point – I'm not looking forward to a pre-transition meatsuit, but I would enjoy a few lifetimes after a transition, if we don't blow up the planet first – either way could be exciting. I was asked to consider a life in this timeframe because I do not have any meatsuits there/then. It is because so many older souls get sidetracked by running into meatsuits from one's own younger higher self. I just wanna hear what they say before I decide if I'm going to join the mission."

Another spirit interjects, "Yeah, that has been a distraction in our efforts: The connection we feel for and unconditional love we have for our own younger-higher-self's meatsuits is so strong that our trust is quite blinding to what they can be up to. I was fucked over by my younger-higher-self only a few meatsuits ago – I was a rich older man and fell for a younger female prostitute. I remember feeling such a connection with her, and gave her gifts and money for twenty ESTC years and it completely distracted me from what I had planned to do that lifetime – I was actually on a previous transition team at the time and completely missed the reminders."

Everyone became quiet with a sense that the meeting was about to begin.

"Okay, everyone is here. Let's plan this thing. It's time to take the ESTC to the next level. We will all meet and remind each other of our primary mission this lifetime and hopefully enough of us will show up to start the transition. As you all know the recent birth control efforts have given us a little reprieve from the potential end of free will, where humans playing ESTC will become a new single minded united life form, much like the hive mind of some insects and larger species. This will be the end of many of the great free-will experiences currently available in the ESTC playground.

"Everyone should pick their DNA, gender and parent type — don't worry if you end up in a religious home because we are including the necessary chromosomes to make it easier to overcome childhood programming or brainwashing and choose your destined path. This childhood exposure to religion will enhance using religion's brainwashing techniques — both musical and non-musical messaging – these skills will come in handy.

"Please include the musical talent DNA set or maybe art or unconventional healing modalities in your meatsuit— please consider this when selecting parents — of course unless you feel called to a different skill set. It's best if we can stay away from situations where we see or hear distractions that will brainwash us too heavily to sense or recognize our mission when reminded of it. Obsessive interest in arts, specifically music, which requires constant attention to be at your desired skill level — this will help minimize negative brainwashing influences which have disrupted our previous efforts to influence global change. We are including expert music talent in many of you — the same set as we used for most every great musician both across time — and I see many of past great musicians here in this meeting – please don't get upset when you aren't sucked into the fame and fortune machine like you were before. In the time frame we are targeting, this talent, in other times, would have pushed many of you into fame and isolation from the masses, but the money grabbers have taken that away from most of the musically talented in the timeframe we are entering.

"We will find ways to get you to where you can befriend many of us, where most can reach the meeting place to re-meet (or re-member) each other for space-time planning and implementation during an annual pilgrimage.

"We will plan and create a new worldwide belief system using techniques mastered by politics, education, commerce and religions to brainwash the general population into believing that they can be happy and live a drama free life with self-brainwashing techniques; while reminding the older souls they are creating reality with their beliefs. This organization will provide great abundance for all of you. Due to the power of the amnesia-effect upon entering a meatsuit, along with the environmental flood of distractive messages, many of you may need up to a year or even two of repetitive positive brainwashing to realize how things do, and have always, worked in the illusion you will call reality, and hopefully you will realize that you are vital to creating this transition.

"We have given you target birth years so most of you will be under 50 rotations during the target timeframe. A small group of you will be going early to enhance the chance that maybe a few of you will remember what's going on down there and with luck remember why.

"I think this is our best chance yet to make this transition. Even though the brainwashing control of the population has never been worse, the ability to collectively impact the whole planet has never been better. Music talent we are sending will allow beliefs to change without effort when the talent here starts writing lyrics to do so. Using the proven methods used by many belief systems, a different type of belief system seems to have a good chance to take off after local young souls are brought in and find the benefits, we think they will find in an unconditionally loving community. Let's make this the spark that brings light the whole planet."

This was the end of the vision. If you are hearing or reading this, you are likely on the transition team. Let me know when you re-member, or re-connect with, your dharma.

Again, the vision above included a reference to the ten billion phenomena. I hear it takes ten billion molecules before a living cell shows signs of life. It takes ten billion brain cells before the brain shows signs of life. Nostradamus predicted the end of humanity as we know it in 2012, but nothing happened – which was not expected given all the predictions he was right about; however, if birth control hadn't become a thing in the twentieth century the population of the planet would have reached ten billion in 2012. Idk if a transition to a single functioning life-form made up from ten billion people would be a bad thing – I used to look forward to 2012, but it is unclear what will happen to the human species except we likely would use more of the brain than we currently do. Giving up free will, Imo, would be a bummer. It's kind of fun to do anything we choose, so maybe we should hold off on populating the planet to ten billion people. I used to think the overpopulation concerns were bullshit, but now wonder if etherealville might be behind that effort to extend the playground life with freewill; but again idk.

I don't get my information in a visual or audio way so everything I get has to be filtered through brain cells that I'm sure are not as good at interpreting my claircognizant source as I would like; and, like everything in this book and the world, it's your job to decide what to believe and why – good luck with that.

REPETITION

Remember nothing is set in stone, and even if it is, the stone is an illusion too.

This transition to global peace in a land of plenty is inevitable – it will eventually happen – be it now or in a couple million years when we do this again, it may be up to you when the transition happens. In order to plan a transition of our species in this earth space-time continuum (ESTC) from fear and external control caused by brainwashing we have been unaware of, that misdirects our creativity, into a playground where we play and have fun and experience each other with open unconditional love and acceptance of all people, and create everything imaginable to help life be the best paradise we can collectively experience, without limits — a world of make believe, a game of make believe. If you are reading this, again, there is a good chance that you, as your Higher Self, were at the same transition meeting of spirits that my Higher Self was at. That's kind of the way this works. Now you get to decide what, if anything, you're going to do about it. Tag, you're it.

FOURTEEN -- CREATING NEW BELIEF SYSTEMS

Episode 14 A New Temporary Belief System

Here are some ideas about how to start a belief system that will take over the world. Yeah, I know that sounds a little ominous; and, technically it may be more like "how to start a temporary belief system that will educate and brainwash the population in order to take back their personal reality, recreating the world, one human at a time" from the influence of those who currently control the narrative, or brainwashing, of the population with repetitive messaging into an undesired illusion of lack and fear in order to control the human population in the ESTC.

I hope we ask ourselves "what is the greatest version of the best vision that I have for reality and how do I intend to help manifest it as it relates to the message in this book?" I currently believe we should start a new belief system as a business with the intention of encouraging positivity and community, while brainwashing and training the population into being happy, drama free and in a state of bliss, and to have fun with others while we are here in these meatsuits.

Before I get too far into the plan for a temporary belief system to start the positive brainwashing of the population, so that we can take over the world, I would like to mention our secret nonviolent weapon. Music. Music is like our secret weapon in "the taking over the world" efforts. It cannot be stopped. Especially once a productive song gets into our heads, where we repetitively hear it in our minds, it becomes a part of our reality. When people start singing it out loud it becomes a part of their personal physical reality. And when it is heard and sung by enough people it becomes a part of our collective reality, changing our world.

All types of music are productive to help create. They already do create. It's just that so many lyrics are not productive and won't be until the lyricist understands the proper way to write grammatically (as described herein) and avoids every reference that we don't want in our reality. Or, put another way, you should write songs to brainwash the listener into believing that life is wonderful, and then life will show up for the listeners just the way that you write the lyrics. This is a big and awesome responsibility for songwriters, once you step on the proverbial bus that is taking us all to wonderland.

This business idea is essentially a temporary belief system, retaining its participation in society by paying taxes so it can voice opinions regarding our reality and heavily influence local and eventually global decision making in addition to all the things below and more. I haven't decided yet on the actual name of the business I desire to create or be a part of – I don't really need to be involved but I know the process well, since I created it, and there are a few ways that one's desires can backfire if we continue talking and thinking the way we have been trained to think and talk our whole lives. The grammar of constructive repetitive messaging is a continuous process as we evolve into the new awareness of what's really going on in this game of make believe that we still think of as reality. The two business names I am considering are "MBC the Make-Believe Church-like-business", or "CULT: Consciousness's Unlimited Literal Truth". As of this writing the two names are interchangeable; but I'm leaning towards the CULT name because it is less confused with the current religious belief system that serves us not. I envision, eventually, a complete transformation of science and education; and the elimination of all billionaires, current religions, and divinations intent on telling people about their future.

MBC/CULT Promotions

Offer promotional services for select local musicians will include helping to book shows and negotiate finances, pairing groups with compatible groups (possibly with common musicians possibly creating new groups). We would also offer special services for songwriters that write positive sing along songs and positive songs (with no mention of things unwanted) with catchy sing along phrases.

I can see promotional services including a full recording studio and everything needed to promote the common goals that we create including concerts, group tours, festivals, etcetera.

MBC/CULT Centers

My vision for a typical community center will include a public music venue, recording studio, indoor and outdoor gathering places for both large and small gatherings suitable for both socializing, education, rituals, etcetera. I can see a metropolis MBC/CULT Community Center evolving to the size of a small community college.

I think we should include care and housing for the poor and/or homeless including day care, other related facilities and food banks, prepared meals along with special needs accommodations. And consider all the extra inclusive ideas that people have – they must include everyone.

MBC/CULT Villages

Hopefully, within one generation, CULT villages will be evolving around the world. A cult village might include a community center, supply locations where everything one needs and desires can be obtained freely, homes for people of all needs and desires, playgrounds and recreation centers for non-competitive games and activities, and anything else that helps people congregate, live free and be happy.

Brainwashing Commercial inside a chapter

This is an emergency commercial interruption of the scheduled regular programming. In your old reality this might initially elevate your concern, igniting fears, but now this type of interruption will just inform you of a little excitement; but often won't actually affect you at all.

Welcome to the make-believe church. I am the grandpa of the church. This is not the first church that I have started. I was the pope of the church of Dabnation (that's d-a-b-nation. We held service at a campground outside the Oregon Country Faire for many years.)

My new church, which is a for profit, capitalist venture, unlike my first church, rather than getting people high with concentrated marijuana products, the goal is to brainwash people into being happy, drama free, and live in a state of near continuous bliss.

Before I get started, I should tell you that I do NOT believe in the concept of a creator that religions seem to promote. The g-word, as used by religions, is not representative of the creative force behind this reality. I prefer the terms Consciousness or Universe to using the g-word. (Oh, and by the way, you are the universe... that's why you named it Universe)

To make it clear, the church I envision starting is NOT a religion— it's closer to an un-religion than a religion. It is a belief system, but it's not like any other belief system that I have observed, in that we are aware of the impact and effect of parasitic beliefs on our reality and the constant brainwashing effect that all belief systems have on us. All other belief systems that I have studied, come with some "truths" that frankly are bullshit and unnecessary — technically they are parasitic beliefs that serve us not and distract us from things that we would like our reality to be.

A short note to old souls before I start with some details of the church including my ideas of monetizing songwriters' income potential:

Old souls may find my ideas about reality useful. But often we reject new ideas until we hear them a few times and then they might start ringing of truth. But many of you are down a path that is actually quite filled with things you really don't want in your reality and some of my ideas have the potential to upset you for one reason or another—this is your shadow. When someone is upset, it is always about oneself. Our Higher Self is trying to tell us something about ourselves that we currently don't know but would be highly beneficial to our spiritual evolution to learn. Often, and as a rule, whatever someone calls another person is always oneself in one way or another – often exactly what we call them.)

Back to MBC Business Plan monetizing ideas.

The primary purpose of the church, again, is to brainwash the general population to become happy and have fun in their reality while enlisting their help to change the world with repetition of focused ideas.

We will promote community building and social acceptance with church services combined with concerts of local artists or MBC community songwriters and their bands (with future touring opportunities).

MBC service-concerts vision would take place in a listening room environment insisting on silence when artists are performing (except singalongs or quality harmony), with no house monetizing inside the venue (merch, food and bar are outside the listening room).

An event example might be, with doors at 0:00 hours, MBC Service starting at 0:30 (and free entry to concert if you are in the door before service start time), first social time break at 01:00, first music set 01:30, next break 02:05, music set 02:30, break 3:05, music 3:30 (last set can go longer if desired), etcetera. Start times for bands will be posted prior to the concert so entry fees can be elevated for closing/premier bands and late entry.

MBC services, for example, would consist of three parts,

1) repetitive brainwashing with affirmations and instructions for a daily personal GAIM Time (Gratitude, Affirmations, Intentions, Meditation), 2) MBC singalong songs, 3) a short message about the beliefs that we encourage.

MBC singalong songs need to be songs that will provide positive catchy lyrics to promote happiness and a make-believe playground that we would like to live in. Songs consist of ONLY words and phrases we want more of in our reality. This is currently rare in songs so we will enlist our friends to write and be reimbursed every time we sing them in an MBC service and the songwriters will retain all rights to privately monetize their songs. (With hopefully a way to produce CDs of just MBC songs from multiple artists for personal brainwashing purposes.) (I see a potential for songwriting competitions with worthwhile prizes and future commissions.)

Monetizing will consist of at least three primary sources:
1) annual church memberships that will include free entry for MBC service-concerts (at any time, even late arrival) and discounts at MBC sponsored festivals and events. The annual membership fee will be something like 0.5% of one's annual income (i.e.: $100,000 = $500). Considering most churches request 10.0% which is twenty times more than we are asking, this seems like a good deal if we have at least two service-concerts per month (100k income would be less than $20 per event).
2) concert entry fees. (Service-concerts are free for early arrivals)
3) passing the plate during the singalong segment of the MBC service.

Musician cuts of profit will be something like this: a) service/ concerts' net income from door take will be split 50-50 between MBC and musicians (+set tips).
b) MBC sponsored listening room concerts; musicians

will receive 74% of net income plus set tips.

c) during an MBC service, MBC songs sung will get x % of the event offering donations from passing the plate and time of event electronic donations (Venmo, cash app, etc.). The songwriter of songs sung will receive y%. If the songwriter is singing the song they get both x% and y% plus z% bonus. (Idk a realistic percentage yet but MBC profit goal is only 26% of net income so hopefully it will be at least a few bucks.)

These are all rough ideas/ proposals and will be modified as needed.

The goal is to create a model that can be propagated to other cities across the planet. This could start with multi day events in specific locations that will provide both service-concerts and other concerts for the musicians (hopefully our peeps along with the new location's local musicians) during concert tours.

Example sermons

Example 1

The brainwashing sermon today begins with breathing. I highly recommend it. Both the process of breathing and the message that I am sharing, from the universe that is available with every breath.

I first heard what I'm about to tell you between twenty and thirty years ago, I don't remember where I heard it or what language it comes from, but it is extremely useful to highlight in one's life, exactly what one is creating with one's beliefs, and one's beliefs are nothing more or less than one's repeated thoughts and repeated words.

The sound of breathing is "ham" for the inhale, and "saw" for the exhale. Ham - saw, ham - saw...

The translation of these words is not required for a positive effect, because our words and thoughts are created in whatever language we speak or think. But for me to make a few points about how to change things, I'll tell you that "ham" means "I am", and "saw" means "that". We are reminding ourselves with every breath that we are "that"— we are whatever we experience or observe in our reality. More specifically, we are creating with our repetitive thoughts and words the beliefs that are turning nothingness into somethingness at each instant.

So, I would like a little audience participation. Let's breath together for a few seconds and gently, on the inhale, say "ham" and think "I am", then, on the exhale, say "saw" while thinking "that".

"I am - that" with every breath. Here we go:

Ham saw ham saw ham saw (keep it going) ham saw I am that I am that I am that I am that.

Again, what is "that"? That is everything you think, see or sense in any way, while you're conscious. This is your real-time reality, in the making.

What if you decide that you don't want "that"?

Sorry, but there is no way to UN-create anything. It's too late, your creations are permanent, forever – so stop trying! Get over it. What you can do is create something new, but you gotta stop thinking and talking about things you do not want in your reality, because that is how it got into your reality. Repeatedly think and say a new reality where you never think or talk about what you don't want more of in your reality. In time, you will no longer notice the things you created in your past when you no longer think or speak of them – your new beliefs will paint over or overwrite your old beliefs– you will have successfully brainwashed yourself into a new reality, like white-washing over your old, no longer serving you, beliefs.

Example 2

Your personal positive brainwashing begins here. I'm going to share with you "the seven affirmations that will improve your life". <have fliers with affirmations on one side and MBC info on other side available to attendees >

Once I said these affirmations out loud for two weeks in a row, my life changed for the better, and with only a few short lapses, I have continued saying them for over a quarter of a century. They are the cornerstone of my daily ritual. I likely wouldn't be where I am now without them. And I really like where I am now — I am currently the happiest I have ever been in this meatsuit. I live a blissful life with amazing friends that I love more than I could ever imagine. I highly recommend being me,

The seven affirmations that will improve your life

say out loud daily

1. My spirit is a field of awareness that connects everything with everything else instantly.

2. My intentions have infinite organizing power.

3. My inner dialogue reflects my inner peace.

4. I know how to go beyond emotional turbulence.

5. I embrace the masculine and the feminine in my own being.

6. Nurturing relationship is the most important thing I can do.

7. I am alert to the opportunity of improbable possibilities.

Say them OUT LOUD every day, at least once. Spaced repetition throughout the day, at least at first, will help you memorize them quickly. It is very important to say them, without changing anything, exactly word for word (every time that I have tried to modify them, I have regretted it and always go back to the original affirmations – if it ain't broke, don't fix it). It is also critical to say them out loud. I highly recommend finding someone that you love and saying the affirmations out loud with them. You can do this in person, if not, over the phone or video chat, works too. If it's in person, once you both know them, it's particularly fun to hug someone for the whole time it takes to say them together (you only need to whisper because your mouths are very close to the other person's ears)– by hugging you get the automatic oxytocin high, to go along with the creative benefits of repeating words and thoughts. Anytime you are in a group, the creative energy is amplified greatly. If you're a singer, you might try to belt them out melodically whenever you warm up your voice – add their energy to your practice or performance – it can't hurt anything.

Thank you.

This is the end of the unexpected commercial interruption by the emergency response team – please return to the episode.

Designing ideas for new belief system

Church model; place with music/speaking venue, place for education, place for positive socializing.

Because we will pay taxes as a business, political activity is allowed including sponsoring local politicians' candidacy for MBC believers as the awareness of how things really work can dramatically improve effectiveness of policies and productive human considerations. (MBC, make believe church-like-business; CULT) The goal is to elect at least two or three candidates for each legislature group, including city council, state and national representatives, state and national senates. Where two or more are gathered, the collective creation force is more than added, it is multiplied; potentially exponentially.

These are just some ideas that seem potentially valuable to propagate positive focused beliefs to effect change. It will be up to you to figure out the best way to create our new reality and this is just one idea, that if it resonates with you, please go for it (and let me help if I'm around).

So, now we need a plan to create focused group affirmations for individuals' happiness and a global intention – just one at a time – to disseminate at concert brainwashing/positive social skills training sessions. And set up music/brainwashing festivals bringing our local musicians to places where we know or have connections and invite their local songwriters/singers to sing in the festival. Depending on the size of the town we could stay more than one day, and our locals will be helped getting gigs in the places we go to also. Please continue this idea, if it seems worthwhile.

Post14.1 Brainwashing Commercial Building Community

Building community is critical to grow

Teaching positive social skills is critical to global transformation. If in the process of teaching people how to be happy and build community, we openly brainwash them with some global ideas like "peace on earth" "nurture relationship" or "abundance for all", it can't hurt anything; and, when enough people are doing this, reality will change.

We could teach them to teach others how to communicate positively in a friendly way. Each new person would be told that everyone here is learning how to teach others how to communicate in a positive, friendly and polite way.

So, how do we communicate in a positive, friendly and polite way? We avoid all complaining about everything. We avoid things we don't want more of in our lives. We learn about body language and how what we physically do attracts communication and interaction. We point out that this community isn't going anywhere. A lot of the same people will be here much of the time, because repetition is how we build happiness and community. Repetition builds community. You start to look forward to seeing people you call friends. Not everyone can be there all the time, but there will usually be at least a few people that you have grown to know, and if not, you can always visit with someone you don't know very well, yet, and you know how to teach the new people very quickly. Before you know it, you will have lots of people that you enjoy hanging out with, which is much nicer than before you started attending the CULT (Community of Unlimited Love Teaching – just a thought).

Promoting social/brainwashing/concerts is a great way to make this possible when we include local singer/songwriters to write positive sing-along songs for the brainwashing session (and also say and promote daily for people to say the 7 Affirmations –maybe get a buddy that you call each day to say them together over the phone – another great way to build positive relationships), and in addition to before and after the brainwashing session have social time in between musical acts also. Music should be in a listening room while the concert part of the event is taking place (when possible, have a separate place where the music could be piped in to hear but away from the performers so people can hear the music, not other people's conversations).

Post14.2 Brainwashing Commercial What now? ...

Here are a few ideas for what one might want to do now:

GAIM Time Ritual daily, maybe with a friend sometimes but always for yourself, whether you know it or not.

Wherever you are, you can start your own CULT social club and maybe there will come along someday a caravan of a group of singers from another town wanting to play their music for you. And you can play your music for them. And, eventually, you will grow to where your community wants to share its music too. Imagine changing the world one community at a time. Why not? What the hell?

Minimizing undesired external brainwashing (turn it off...).

Post 14.3 The Final Brainwashing Commercial
Repetition

Allow me to repeat the big red X of the simple truths one more time: think and talk only of things you desire more of in your reality.

Repetition is all you need to create whatever you can imagine. Repeat it over and over until it is real – this is the way this game works. So, you may find it useful to read this book over, and over and over... If you really want to amp it up, read it out loud. In a way, this book is like things that many of us binge watch now, with or without commercial interruptions; please be encouraged to binge read this book at least once a year, the more the merrier; after all, Repetition creates.

The end

AUTHOR'S AFTERWORD

Appreciation for Others' Work/Ideas

The following wonderful people helped brainwash me into what I am today. (So, blame them, not me. Haha)

Conversations with God, books one and two; by N.D. Walsch.

Your Body's Many Cries for Water; by F. Batmanghelid.

7 Agreements; (sometime last century), I heard from Deepak Chopra.

Beliefs; YouTube; by Abraham Hicks.

Illusions; by R. Bach.

The Four Agreements; by D. Ruiz.

Other Stuff That Might Be Useful

This is stuff that I'm sticking in here at the last minute, because you just never know when you're gonna have the opportunity to put your foot in your mouth as I may do from time to time – in other words, I am capable of changing my mind on anything and/or everything if my inner message changes. (However, if I later deny everything that is in this book, and say it was a joke, someone paid me a lot of fucking money to say it. haha)

The thing that I am finding is that this mishmash of life

REPETITION

that I've led seems to have prepared me for the path ahead, be it peddling a book and new belief system by busking or talking with people (and speaking or recording my message to people); whatever the future brings will be fun and entertaining, I'm sure. Why the fuck not, for christ sake? I'm making my reality just like you are, and I supposedly know what I'm doing.

One of the things I'm thinking about writing is a fiction story set in the future that tells of a guy that had to hide in the south american wilderness for twenty years (pays to have friends) and by then the house of cards that was reality had mostly all tumbled and they no longer wanted to find and incarcerate him or worse. But he was having the time of his life in a paradise of natural medicines and good food and people, helping build community the best way he could. He had people willing to insist he do the things to maintain good health taking care of an older meatsuit. (It would be an honor to help tumble the proverbial house of cards that our reality currently is.)

Idk if I've said it ten times already but I don't expect a large percentage of the population finding what I'm writing as useful as I think it is; but, if enough people take it seriously and propagate the concepts to new generations, I think we will see wonderful things from young humans brainwashed differently than they are now. (I just happened upon something that had a ring of truth to it, a finding that intelligence is decreased and stabilized as a result of the current education we receive, when intelligence without education grows naturally and far more rapidly. But we will never hear of this again if what usually happens happens again – where existing methods imply incompetence rather than welcoming improvements.) (I will admit I am on a roll with this current rambling. Perhaps you should just go read the book if this is too upsetting, but you probably already bought the darn thing so maybe... just jump over to chapter 1 and come back and finish this later if you wish.)

DOYLEMOORE

I think there is some amazing shit in here, but fuck, what do I know? After all, I am technically making all this up, out of thin air, as they say.

One thing to be aware of, regarding the world conditions big red X: Half of every dollar you spend goes to the 8 richest billionaires. The other side of this is your income; and absolutely none of your income comes from the 8 richest billionaires. This may sound a little extreme, but I intend the richest billionaires all transform into charitable organizations giving away 90% or more of what they make to help everyone be and live free, or they all just disappear, and their money magically gets distributed to those who need it. (I know. That intention is too long, but you know what I mean.)

Instead of using the human population to create wealth for a few, we will use the human population to create abundance and happiness for all. Yes, of course, by brainwashing ourselves into believing it.

There can sometimes be hidden beliefs behind our conscious chosen belief. An example is if you say and know better that there is no merit in what I am saying about certain things or even everything I'm saying, but there are certain things I say that have a "ring of truth" to it, or even you wish something I'm saying were true but you don't know for sure and have no evidence either way, well I say what would it do to say okay, "I'll choose to believe it for now until someone laughs at me" (don't tell anyone the new beliefs, but do so without lying, i.e.. "I'm collecting data for a physics experiment") until you see results and find value in the processes. That is the way EVERY belief system works, including the ones you have now. Yes, whatever you know to be so is likely a brainwashing from one source or another, because as soon as you know what they're telling you is truth, it will be the truth for you – that's how everything works -- your thoughts and words make them so for

REPETITION

you. Belief systems require your energy (and money) to exist. So, you might as well consciously choose to believe something that, if it were a truth, this would be a better universe, a better reality (or at least try it out – you can always change your mind). I highly recommend everyone try it out to create a life of happiness and bliss, collect your own data and modify the model presented here and create your own model of reality. If you ever don't like where you went with your model, you can always come back here and start again. (I've done this a few times already, that's why I recommend what I'm describing in this book.)

And did I mention that I am fucking done with this fucking book and that's the one thing I didn't go into the detail that I should have, fucking. Fucking, and I don't mean just coitus but anyway two or more people physically contact each other for the express purpose of each person having a good orgasm, is the most fun we can have in our bodies, pleasurably utilizing all physical senses. We should do this a lot more than we do. (I mean, after all, since life is an illusion for the purpose of experiencing other life forms like ourselves in the most positive experiences we can, fucking is possibly the best thing we can do – it seems like fear-based brainwashing is likely responsible for some people not fucking as much as they can and coming to the conclusion that you are an eternal being and nothing can actually harm you or anyone, than it would seem less of a need to fear much of what we are brainwashed to fear.) It's hard to be brainwashed by a media storm when you are fucking, and again, not when you are just being fucked – yes, you can watch TV while getting fucked, but stop watching TV altogether as soon as possible; so that you can keep fucking as much as possible and turning off the constant flow of bullshit into the brain, I believe both fucking and fearlessness are positive goals while in a meatsuit.

And one really good reason to have a good time when your fucking is the past life review. It's where after we go home, we get to experience our whole life again through the full senses, thoughts and feelings of every other person we have affected. So, if you are an inconsiderate male and simply stick your dick in some soft hole, and be done in a few minutes, or less, and your partner is thinking what a fucking waste of time, and she's thinking why didn't I choose that older gentleman who might even give a shit about what I'm experiencing, but, no, pick the cute punk who can't fuck worth a shit – when will I learn. Anyway, fellow, when you kick the bucket, you get to experience what she is going through while you are prematurely climaxing. On the other hand, she is going to get to experience your orgasm after she goes home, so at least she will get a little something pleasurable out of the after-experience. So anyway, the point is to enjoy it so the other person will get to enjoy it when they go home too. Whoever you're with, do whatever you can to heighten their enjoyment, that's all I'm saying.

My goal is to brainwash the reader into believing the following:

That every externally imposed repetitive thought and word we have experienced is brainwashing us into believing what we experience as reality.

When conscious, you are the one and only consciousness with full access to all unlimited creative abilities.

That there is nothing real in what we experience as reality, and this illusion that we experience is all the product of our creative consciousness.

This life we are all living is actually a pseudo-reality game of make believe that we are playing with our Self.

That consciousness is the source of both our experience and our creation.

The purpose of life is to be happy and have fun with others.

That you made a plan before this lifetime to help transform the earth space time continuum into the abundant, loving, and peaceful pseudo-reality it has always meant to be and inevitably will be.

And you are more than you have ever imagined.

Needing to point out how something used to be worse than it is now, is how you move back in time to make things worse. Point out how something is "better now" not "worse than before" and do so without mentioning what was "worse".

Holidays and Special Months are not useful for two reasons: they usually want to highlight an undesirable distinction in the past, and to have a "special" day implies every day isn't potentially the best day of your life. Holiday comes from Holy Day, which was a way to keep people interested in something lest they forget all about it. I think every day should be and is, if we let it be, a holy day.

One very useful technique for brainwashing a population into believing something completely made up is to say it from multiple sources, repeatedly.

One very useful technique for brainwashing a population into believing something completely made up is to say it from multiple sources, repeatedly.

One very useful technique for brainwashing a population into believing something completely made up is to say it from multiple sources, repeatedly.

To practice positive socializing skills, when we realize that our repetitive thoughts and words are creating our personal and collective realities, it is crucial to re-learn how to communicate with others for many people with habits of telling everyone about something they obviously do not want more of in their reality. I know many people that I currently just walk away from at the earliest convenience to avoid hearing what they are saying that I don't want more of in my reality

Sarcasm becomes you

What are your beliefs now? How can you tell? Look at your reality, look at the world you live in. You can only observe the creative results of your beliefs, many of which you may not want more of in your future. You can control your repetitive thoughts and words.

I believe that there are no accidents and this whole game is planned out by our higher selves, or, in other words, we are doing all this shit to ourselves, but we took the amnesia pill and don't realize (or remember) that we agreed to or chose to experience exactly what we actually experience here.

Einstein quote: "Imagination is everything. It is the preview of life's coming attractions."

There are no problems, there are only opportunities. Focus on the shortest, simplest path to the desired outcome. Do not say "problem", say "opportunity". Focus on solutions but try not to overuse that word either – we do not desire to deal with finding solutions, we desire to have a perfect end result, consistently, repeatedly.

Avoid competition at all costs, in all ways. Encourage collaboration and sharing of ideas and suggestions for the best path to the end result. Discuss the ideas, focusing on the simplest, easiest routes first that meet the most significant variable in the process. Everyone should agree upon the simplest path, even if at first, we think another path is simplest, if so, repeatedly affirm out loud that the collective's determined simplest path will succeed. ...

For process improvements envision the simplest solution working and look for evidence that an improved outcome is possible using this recommended process change. (And know that the evidence you observe is the creation of your beliefs which are nothing more or less than your repeated thoughts and words; keep saying them and find more and better evidence that the most significant improvement will likely improve many, if not all, undesired opportunities in the process imagineering improvement. Continuing affirmative rhetoric until everyone

REPETITION

fervently knows it, and the universe must make it so, for everyone that does know it.

Rather than using statistics to calculate likelihood or probabilities, use graphing and view the information while developing a process or process improvement as a tool to an inevitable outcome better than you had imagined. Envision and imagine the outcome, repeatedly, (within a unified collective for even faster results) and then look for evidence, continue the imagined outcome enough and evidence will appear. Observe your created evidence and modify your imagined outcome as needed, and repeat. Evidence will confirm your creation and upon believing it, results will appear until you know that it is so. So be it.

Some examples of things we might like to "imagineer" into existence include the following, but the list is limited only by your imagination.

No maintenance, self-powered, 1-million-mile cars. (Maybe with on-board nuclear, wind, sun, and/or electric powered motors designed like the original electric car experiment in the city of Sacramento CA in the 1980's. Also, tires made of semi-truck rubber will not need to be replaced. It's worth realizing that cars are currently designed to and make far more money for maintenance and repair than the actual sale of the car. This can happen.)

Buildings made of mushrooms and hemp-Crete that are earthquake proof and will last 10,000 years with little or no maintenance.

If we don't watch the news than we are not personally bothered by world events. Try it. It's very worthwhile as far as the influence it has on our reality. And I contend that it is better to live ignorant of many things and be happy rather than worry about something that literally doesn't change my local reality at all. And, have no expectations, and every day enjoy it but fear not if it is the last day and know that we just go home when

215

the meatsuit stops working. I would rather be happy than worry about something I personally have no control over. We will create a reality of peace and plenty, inevitably

Made in the USA
Monee, IL
12 October 2024

67131824R00125